Far Beyond What We Can See

Supernatural Encounters... Life Beyond the Hereafter

Bev. Duffey-Martin, Ph.D, D.Min.

PETTIS PUBLISHING
Dayton
New York

Library of Congress Cataloging-in-Publication Data

Martin, Beverly, Far Beyond What We Can See

ISBN 978-164316701-5

Pettis Publishing Inc.
1022 Terracewood Drive
Englewood, Ohio 45322
cspettis1975@gmail.com
937-477-6441

Cover Design: Nashon Duffey and Dr. Beverly Martin

Design and Layout: Carmen Gaines and Curtis Pettis

Edited by: Rosalind Osinubi, Vicki Pettis and Curtis S. Pettis

Editorial Team: Chris Pettis and Nicole Pettis

Printed in the United States of America

Dedication and Appreciation

Praise to my Father God, Jesus, my Lord and Savior, and the Holy Spirit, my guide, whom without, I have no story.

I am grateful for my soulmate, Dr. Truman Martin--a divine hookup (as shared in this publication). I am grateful that he encourages me to fulfill my own destiny and not just be an "attachment" to his purpose only. I also dedicate this book to my five "T's" (my rays of sunshine): Tranisha, Trenton, Tre'Von, Trushana, and Travarus, along with my son-in-love, Doug and my daughter-in-loves, Kanule and Raychelle; Me-Maw's little peeps: Xaivera, Brennen, Amaya, Aiden, Karis, the twins: Zoie and Zyan, Laquinn, Alaiya and Ray Lynn who will arrive soon. I can't mention my peeps without smiling.

I also dedicate this book to the greatest church in the world, my church family, Maranatha Worship Centre of Dayton, OH. I sincerely appreciate you!

Acknowledgement

I must first acknowledge my father, Bishop Nathaniel Duffey, Sr., and my mother, Evangelist Lucille Duffey and my youngest sister, Sabrina who are presently residing at 312 Golden Street in Pearly Gates County, Heaven. I'm grateful for the godly principles, morals, integrity, character and love they shared and instilled within me. My parents taught me to follow Christ--not to mention their prayers that never ceased, but are still pushing me, my sister Evangelist Darl; brother, Rev. Dr. Nathaniel; grandchildren, nieces, nephews and loved ones to our destiny. I also acknowledge my mother-in-"love", Missionary Ormie Martin, who has been a Prayer Warrior General for me and my family.

I would be remiss not to mention a few persons who paved the way; wearing "sandals" that I might wear "shoes", Big Mama and Big Daddy Williams, who pointed me towards Christ and showed me love in action, Mother Hayman, Pastor Doris Swartz, Ernestine Lenoir, Dr. Juanita Smith, my aunts, Daisy, Florence, Rubye, Lucille, and Uncle MC. When I envision their faces, they seem to make heaven real and point me towards Heaven's door, along with the others too numerous to name.

Special thanks to my prayer partners and spiritual path directors: my sister, Darl; Godsisters: Diane and Rose—each of these ladies are powerful ministers. Thanks to my prophetic daughters and sons and spiritual mentors Dr. Ruth White, Evangelist Ralphena Dodson, and Prophet-Pastor Garnett S. Greer. Space does not allow me to mention everyone that has helped me on my journey. I love you all.

Table of Contents

Foreword
By
Prince Maurice Parker, Th.D.

Humanly speaking, I met my sister Rev. Beverly Martin in, what I would call, a random, round-about way. Around 2009, I received a letter at my home in Spain from some Christian sisters from the San Francisco Bay area informing me that they were doing a genealogical investigation on their family tree and found that I was related to them, something to the tone of fourth cousins, via my maternal grandfather. One of the sisters was Phillis Duffy-Johnson, the wife of Bishop Clarence Johnson. They asked if they could visit me to Spain to get to know me and my family.

I loved the idea, because there is so much about my family that I do not know, and for decades I thought that I was the only Christian in my family. My family thought that I was mad and had wasted my life that held such academic promise. (I had graduated from high school in 1971 with a full-ride scholarship to an Ivy League university*). As a result, my immediate family had cut me off shortly after my conversion and held me like a pariah.

On my own, it took me years of hard work to finally complete my grad school education while serving on the mission field, and I was able to receive my doctorate in theology having studied in Trinity Theological Seminary and Canterbury Christ's Church, in Canterbury, England. My family held no appreciation for my Christian ministerial vocation, aspirations and educational endeavors because they did not consider it a serious, worthwhile career choice. They also felt that it was below them and in rejection of all their efforts to help me "make something" of my life.

After nearly fifty years in active ministry, more than 45 of them (at the time of this writing) living on the mission field as one of the few African-American career cross-cultural foreign missionaries. For more than fifteen years I lived in the jungles, mountain villages and cities of Latin America and the Caribbean planting churches where there was no Gospel-Believing Christian witness. We planted more than 20 churches in those areas. As an army brat, I was raised in Western Europe, and in 1982, the Lord spoke to me that I would return to Europe to preach the Gospel that I never heard while I lived there. I have been serving, principally, in Spain since 1988.

Therefore, after all these years, I was thrilled to find that I was biologically related to other Believers that loved the Lord!

The following year, I was in Los Angeles, California, when I received a call from Sister Phillis who informed me that another cousin, Dr. Beverly

Martin, was also in Los Angeles on ministerial business and wanted to meet me. We did meet and immediately bonded in spirit.

Not long after that, I received another phone call at my home in Spain from Dr. Truman Martin, my cousin Beverly's husband. He was on his way to Ghana, Africa, for one of his frequent medical/preaching mission trips and wanted to stop by to visit us for a day in Spain on his way back home. I picked him up at the airport in Seville and took him to our seminary when he preached a Pentecostal sermon like I think that few of those young Spanish ministerial candidates had ever heard!

Since then, we have so partnered in ministry and built a family bond that I have ministered in their church, The Maranatha Worship Centre, in Dayton, Ohio. Dr. Bev has even brought her youth Hip-Hop dance group to bless and minister in the churches here in Córdoba and Seville, Spain, and we maintain communication on a regular.

As per Dr. Bev (as I lovingly call her), my relationship with her and this book is concerned, since the time that I receive Christ, I have buried every member of my immediate family. I am the lone survivor. Some of them came to find the everlasting hope in Christ, and for some, I can only hope for as much.

Nevertheless, with the passing of each one, there was a definite supernatural spiritual experience that surrounded their passing. Many times, I have sat back stroking my beard thinking, "Wow! Now THAT was interesting!" as I pondered the peculiar situations at their passing. I am sure that God was in the works somewhere beyond that which I could physically detect with my five natural senses.

I can say that Dr. Bev is writing this essay based on her experience with the subject matter, her experience in the Word and her love and passion to minister life, love and spiritual health to all with whom she comes into contact. These words are born from a lifetime of zealous service, church, and ministerial experience that she possesses which is impressive enough but would mean nothing without her dauntless and passionate love for our Lord Jesus Christ!

She is constantly busy in service to others and the ministries of the church both locally and nationally. I have loving dubbed Dr. Bev one of the busiest, hardest working woman in ministry. Sometimes, when I talk to her during our regular phone conferences, she has usually just come in from somewhere, or on her way to somewhere else. I jokingly think, "Is the Dr. Bev moniker just an abbreviation for Dr. Busy as a Beaver?"

After reading this book, I have discovered that the heartache of the pain of the loss of a loved one has not been a stranger to her. However, those eyes that have shed so many tears because of the loss of a loved one, smile and shine glowingly with all naturality from the depth of a soul which Christ has made as His ever welcome and permanent abode.

This book is based on her personal experiences with God's victories over the brevity of life, of those things seen and unseen, known and unknown, dreams and visions and how we should properly handle them. Though it speaks much of that which we know as death, it speaks much more of the hope of our life in Christ and eternal life and this fleeting, temporal life here on Earth.

I pray that it blesses and ministers to you in the most profound way.

H.M.S.,
Dr. Prince Maurice Parker
Vice Dean of International Affairs
Professor of Old Testament History.
Exegetics, and Apologetics
Assemblies of God Theological Seminary
(Facultad de Teología – FADE)
Assemblies of God of Spain
La Carlota, Córdoba, Spain

Endorsements

Far Beyond What I Can See is captivating from the first paragraph. Dr. Martin has an incredible gift of explaining the supernatural and the natural in such a practical and relatable fashion. She is a woman who is captivated by the supernatural power of God and wholly committed to Him. This book will give you insight, peace, and revelation and is especially powerful for those who have lost loved ones and hope. God's grace is sufficient and he is always faithful. This book is an answer to your prayer - a must read. I sincerely thank God for her gift and for sharing her with the body of Christ. The word says that we should prosper and be in health as our soul prospers - this book will speak to your soul and cause it to prosper.

Joedrecka S. Brown Speights, MD
Tallahessee, FL

The Sovereignty of God is clearly depicted throughout this latest release by Dr. Beverly J. Martin. Like any good book of anticipation, "Far Beyond What We Can See," will keep you wondering, "What's next?" You will undergo a frenzy of emotions causing you to laugh, get angry, cry, then shout unto God with a voice of triumph! By the end, you will be convinced: ***GOD IS SOVEREIGN!***

Annjanette C. Foster, M.S.
Dayton, OH

Dr. Beverly Martin is an aspiring leader, motivator and teacher who often uplifts everyone that she comes in contact with! I've had multiple instances upon which after speaking to her about life after death and supernatural occurrences, I left with chills. After nearly experiencing death herself, she has very insightful revelation on what happens in the world around us that we cannot see. I believe that anyone who wants to know more about what you can expect after your journey here should read this book and be built up in faith and knowledge concerning the life after this one.

Pastor Gerald A. Johnson
Gerald A. Johnson Ministries
Faith Culture Church
Round Rock, TX 78664

Far Beyond What We Can See" takes readers on a trail of hope, comfort, and confirmation for their loved ones who have transitioned from life as we know it, to the life that God promised.

Tranisha M. Misenheimer
Austin, TX

Introduction

CHAPTER 1

Beyond What I Could See

I boarded the plane in a blur. As I walked, it seemed as if my feet were barely touching the ground. Mom had come to visit 38 days earlier. While my children were in school, it was going to be an enjoyable mother-daughter bonding time, so I thought. My husband was scheduled to leave for Africa on a mission trip two days after her arrival.

I tried to make sense of this blur. "Lord, how could such a delightful plan turn so sour?" This whole whirlwind started when Mom had a stroke on the airplane on her way to visit me. Mom had been an otherwise healthy woman in her early 70's. Despite this, seemingly not so serious health crisis, her prognosis was optimistic. Doctors established a plan for her to go through a brief rehab, then return home to California. But this all changed when she developed a blood clot and matters got worse.

As I looked into Mom's face that Monday morning, she went into a cold stare. Suddenly, my world stood still. I was suspended in time. Sadly, I watched my mom take her last breath. "NO, GOD! NOT MY MOM!" The medical staff whisked me out of the room while they tried to resuscitate her. I was placed in a room next door where I fell into a heap on the floor. I spoke into the atmosphere, "Mom, you must return into your body! We need you! Dad needs you! God, you must bring Mom back! You promised in Your Word, if we would ask, it would be given…Seek, and I would find… Knock, and the door would be opened! God, I'm doing that!" In the midst of my emotional storm, I heard laughter coming from the room next door where they were trying to resuscitate Mom. The staff came to tell me, "We got her back!" But what seemed like seconds later, they lost her heartbeat again. My heart dropped. As I petitioned God, "Please don't let me down!" this yo-yo experience occurred twice more. The last time when I went down to my knees to pray, I heard Mom's voice in my spirit say, "I just came back to tell you that I LOVE YOU." Although, I was sad and hurt, I immediately felt peace. Jehovah Shalom, the peace of God, hit me from the top of my head down to my feet. Yes, tears flowed from my eyes, but that overwhelming, all-consuming, deep grief did not overtake my soul. There was a peace in the midst of my storm. **HALLELUJAH!**

After processing the fact that Mom had transitioned and making a phone call to my husband, I was faced with a bigger mountain. How would I tell my dad, who was in California, that his wife of 50 years was gone? This task seemed insurmountable. But, beyond what we can see, there is an all-knowing God who is omnipotent (having unlimited power), and omnipresent (present everywhere – at the same time).

When I finally made that dreadful call, my sister picked up the phone and helped me by saying, "I was awakened from a dream where I saw Mom dancing on stage and I was encouraging her to stay on stage but she said, "No! You do it, Darl." (advising her to dance in her stead). When she awakened, she sensed that Mom was leaving so she got up from her bed, dressed, and awaited my call to confirm it. My sister offered her assistance to inform Dad that Mom had passed. Unbeknownst to me at the time, a few hours earlier, Dad told my sister that he had had a dream concerning our mom. In his dream, Mom was going up an escalator. He called out to her to come back but she would not turn around. Dad said he felt that she would not be returning. With sadness and tears in his eyes and despite his prayers, her transition had taken place.

In spite of the pain of losing her, I stayed to spend time with Mom's body. Even though it made no sense in my mind, I felt the comfort of her words by letting me know that she loved me. Suddenly a chair in the shower area began to move, but I did not fear. I knew Mom was now more alive than she ever was! Hebrews 12:1a tells us "Wherefore seeing we also are compassed about with so great a cloud of witnesses…" (KJV). It tells us that our loved ones are beckoning us to run this spiritual race that is set before us. (See Chapter 6 ~ Spiritual Awareness). In my spirit I knew that it was well with her soul. Beyond what I could see with my natural eyes or hear with my natural ears, she was more alive than ever! Her last breath here was her first breath in the presence of God. Beyond what I could see had become a reality to me.

CHAPTER 2

My First Point of Awareness

I asked myself, "When was my first point of awareness that there was a world that was outside or beyond what I could see?" I recalled a time when I was approximately seven years old when my maternal grandmother, "Big Mama," who I thought was a wonderful, older grandmother; (however, looking back she was only in her mid-forties), told us about a vision. Big Mama had lost in infancy a son, L.C., that I never knew. Of course, I knew her other children, Uncle M.C., Mom, Aunt Florence and Aunt Daisy. That day, Big Mama began talking about her son, L.C. that died from pneumonia when he was eight months old. She spoke of how much he looked like "Dear" (My Mom's nickname), and bragged of how smart L.C. was as a baby. Big Mama spoke of how she cried a lot and missed her baby daily after he died. However, she said one night she awoke and saw an image of him sitting on her dresser, but she was

5

not afraid. He was cooing, smiling, and appeared happy. She knew that he was at peace. She looked forward to the day that she would see him again in heaven and could hold him in her arms. I imagine that upon Big Mama's passing at age 70, she was greeted by Baby L.C., and lovingly held him in her arms just as she had imagined. I believe that hearing Big Mama's experience triggered my curiosity of "The Beyond." My Grandmother also told us that she was born with a "veil over her face" (also known as a Caul Birth). It occurs when a piece of the amniotic sac remains attached to the baby's head upon delivery. In the southern part of the USA, some cultures believe that a baby born with this caul will have a special destiny or psychic abilities. Though she deemed her baby son L.C.'s visitation as a positive occurrence, she deemed some other encounters as satanic. Big Mama was a strong believer in Jesus Christ. She never walked in fear and would take authority over any adverse spirits that came toward her, in the name of Jesus! Late one night when I went to Sacramento with her to visit her sister, I heard her speaking to a spirit in a dark room between our room and the bathroom. She commanded, "You must go! Get out of here now!" She admonished the spirit and exclaimed, "We are covered by the blood of Jesus and you must leave in Jesus' name!"

As a child, I had a strong fear of death. I believe it came about at age five when I went to a funeral with my family. It was the funeral of a pastor that had died of a heart attack. I had met this pastor prior to his passing. When I saw the painful emotional responses of others it alarmed me. Another pastor passed shortly thereafter and I was traumatized once again, to say the least. I asked my family, "What if they wake up in that box down in that hole?"

Watching scary movies like "Frankenstein" did not ease my emotions but only escalated my fears of death. As a joke, my Dad would take his guitar and play songs like "I'll Fly Away" or "When the Saints Go Marching In." I would begin screaming and falling out. I felt like I was being smothered but could not voice my fears. Mom, realizing that I was truly traumatized by these antics and that I wasn't being a drama queen, asked Dad to stop playing such songs related to death in my presence. By the time Dad realized that I was truly upset and horrified, the damage was done. The template was set and the fear of death gripped me for several years.

I could not attend my Godmother's funeral no matter how much the family wanted me there. When my family went to a funeral viewing I stood back by the door and would not step fully inside.

Nightmares plagued me until I was 13 years old. I remember vividly what broke the fear. Our twin friends Tommy and Shirley's little sister, Laverne Joy, was hit by a car only a few blocks from us and killed instantly. It was devastating to the family, the school, and neighborhood. By that time I was a young keyboard player and singer. I was asked to share music at Laverne Joy's Homegoing Service. The fear that I once had related to death tried to return but I did not want to disappoint my friends by not following through with my assignment at the Homegoing. I pushed myself to go and I viewed the little girl's body prior to the funeral. She looked so peaceful and just like a beautiful sweet doll dressed in pink. The fear was broken and I was no longer afraid.

Less than a year later another friend's sister, Beverly Diane, died after she was hit by a car while riding her bike. I also played music for her Homegoing Service. From that day forward, I began to see that we live in a body but our soul and spirit (inner man), belong to God. I was happy to realize that our spirit and soul man does not die. I then understood that when we give our hearts to God we can live forever.

What Truly Triggered The Fear?

I am grateful that God helped me manage my fear and I was able to move past it. I would, however like to explore cause and effect. Were the funerals of those pastors and the "TV monsters" the real cause of this fear? I will admit these negative experiences did play a major role in my fear and anxiety; however, there were also two other situations that influenced my fear.

At that time the only Black funeral home in Bakersfield, California was one street behind where I lived. Rucker's Mortuary was owned by Mr. Samuel Del Rucker. Mr. Rucker and his wife were friends of my parents and grandparents who lived next door to the mortuary. The Rucker family lived in a residence above the business like in the movie "My Girl". Our backyard and the mortuary were separated by a black wire fence. Earlier one afternoon, Mom had hung clothes out on our clothesline to dry. It was almost dusk and she asked me to go out and gather the clothes from the line. I will admit that I had an attitude because she was interrupting my television show but I knew better than to display my annoyance with my mother: (Lucille didn't play!).

Episode One: As I was taking the clothes down from the line I noticed a man in a black

9

suit coming from the direction of the mortuary toward the black wire fence. I began slowly moving towards the house. While gathering the clothes, I did not see where he had actually come from but I thought, "There's no way he can catch me because he has to climb over the fence, and by that time I can run into the house." His pace and stride were steady. He got to the fence, but did not climb over it. Instead he walked right through it then disappeared on my side of the fence! I ran as fast as my legs could carry me into the house screaming, "Mama! Mama!" Needless to say, it was a wrap!

Episode Two: I spent the night with my Aunt Lucille, her husband and their eight children. It was fun to be with my cousins (4 boys; 4 girls), who lived right next door. We girls decided to put on bed sheets and go into the boys' room and scare them. I was in the front of the line when we tip-toed down the hall, one behind the other. Midway down the hall we were stopped by a man so tall that his head and top hat touched the ceiling! He was dressed in all black and as I faced him and looked up, he looked down. We all made an about face and ran back to the girls' room. We jumped into bed one by one without a sound and hid beneath the covers. Someone finally broke the silence, "Did you see that man?" We did not come out of the room until morning. Just like there are wonderful angelic hosts, there are also demonic hosts. **Ephesians 16:12** tells us: *"For we wrestle not against flesh and blood, but against principalities, against powers, and the rulers of the darkness of this world, against spiritual wickedness in high places."* (KJV).

I am thankful for God's saving grace. I am grateful that God gave me power to overcome fear and to have a heart to seek after Him. I am thankful to God for parents that did not live a double standard. They were not perfect but they led by example. My parents believed in training up children in the way they should go and going that way themselves.

Moving From Childhood Fear to Teen Reality

One afternoon, during a three o'clock church service, a very poised sister of the church was praising God. Suddenly, she did something strange and out of her normal character. She fell to her knees, crawled down the floor towards the altar, and went back and forth in front of the pulpit three times while everyone just looked on in astonishment! She said the words, "Sadness! Sadness! Sadness!" Then she got up with tears in her eyes and returned back to her seat. My best friend LaWanda was sitting next to me during that service. Just six days later we were involved in a car wreck and LaWanda, tragically died. Later, we realized that the area where the church sister had been exclaiming "Sadness!" was where my best friend would lie in a coffin several days later. If you have read my book: **"Winning! By God's Grace in satan's Face"**, you know that this was the car wreck that changed my life.

We were coming back from a musical in Fresno, California where our singing group had ministered. I was with three of my teenage friends (members of our singing group), a close male friend, (who was driving my car), and my brother Nathaniel. The last thing I remember prior to the crash was a sign that read "Bakersfield 39 Miles." I thought to myself, "We'll be home soon."

I was sitting in the front middle seat next to my brother. My brother recanted later that as the car flipped four times he saw me moving as if I would exit the car through the front window but he grabbed me to prevent that from occurring. When the car landed all the windows except the one on the driver's side were broken out and the car's motor was on the pavement. It was totaled. My best friend, LaWanda, had been sitting in the middle seat in the back. LaWanda died instantly that night. I also visited the chambers of death and nearly died. I broke my neck in the accident, was partially paralyzed, and had a concussion. My Brother and the car's other occupants were alive but all had scratches and bruises. It was a blur. Paramedics took LaWanda in the first ambulance then Ann and me in the second. I could hear Ann crying. The ambulance attendant pulled the covers up around my neck as I drifted into another dimension. I could no longer hear Ann crying, nor the sounds of the ambulance. That place was dark and cold (spiritually cold). I wanted to say, "But, I've been in church!" But I knew that "church" could not save me and would not take the place of a relationship with Christ. Like the sinner on the cross, I asked for another chance. God spoke words to me that I will always remember: ***"I'll give your life back to you, and see what you do with it?"*** Then I returned into my body and once again could hear Ann crying.

Mom later admitted that they considered holding Lawanda's body a little while longer before her funeral so they would not have to have two funerals, in case I didn't make it. But I knew that God had given me more time. He had given me another opportunity to fulfill my destiny and walk out my purpose, beyond what my natural eyes could see.

Even with ministry obligations at this season in my life and being a mom and grandmother, I can never move past the mission God has given me, and the heart to reach out and embrace teenagers, and young adults.

I co-pastor a church with my husband and on July 23, 2016, one of our church youth, Mason, age 12, had a supernatural experience. Mason rode his new bike to our Christian Hip-Hop dance rehearsal at the church. After rehearsal he proceeded to ride home. As he rode into a crosswalk on the highway a car clipped the back of his bike. It knocked him into the road and he was then run over by a motorcyclist. He lay in the street bleeding from the head with both arms injured and broken which later required surgery. Mason said it happened so fast that he did not even remember the impact. He stated that all he remembered was floating in the atmosphere and looking down wondering what all these people were looking at. He then saw himself lying in the street in a puddle of blood! He saw his mentor and cousin, Associate Pastor Al Phillips, and said, "Al, I'm O.K.!" By the grace of God, Mason was able to return into his body. We all, including Mason, now know that God has a plan for him beyond what he can see.

CHAPTER 3

Supernatural Premonitions
(You Can't Explain?)

Years came and went. One December my Mom lost her youngest sister, my Aunt Daisy, and was deeply grieved. The following May, my dad wanted to cheer Mom up by purchasing her the "car of her dreams" for Mother's Day, (Although, we found out later, the car was actually "Dad's dream car" and not Mom's - LOL!). Dad asked us kids to help with the gift and we all did our part to help make it happen. Mom appreciated that big new car.

In June, we went to Disney World to celebrate my nephew Dywren's high school graduation. Mom and Dad joined us at a couple of theme parks in Florida, but mostly enjoyed just sitting out on the hotel's balcony taking in Florida's beautiful sunshine. I can still remember seeing Mom cleaning off the patio table as if she were cleaning at home. My sister and I, along with our kids, went to the theme parks to enjoy the rollercoasters. After that trip, Mom and Dad followed up with a cruise of their own. This was not unusual for my dad. Despite being a pastor and state church leader, he always made time for his family. Even in the years of financial challenge during our upbringing, we were still blessed with family camping trips or something fun.

After our Florida vacation and Mom and Dad's cruise my sister told me about a strange vision she had in September. My sister lived next door to our parents. One day she was at their house in a room where she often stayed while visiting. She heard the doorbell ring and our Dad called out, "Darl, get the door." Upon opening the door she saw a pink looking coffin but refused to look into it to see who was inside. She headed back to the room where she had been. As she passed by my parent's room she saw Dad sitting on the right side of the bed but did not recall seeing Mom. The vision was unsettling but she kept praying and interceding about it. She did not feel led to share it with others, including me, as it was very disturbing...to say the least.

In October, I had to have a surgical procedure for which I had to stay overnight in the hospital. I had a disturbing dream during the night. In my dream I saw a dark coffin with roses made into its corners. I immediately got worried and began to pray asking God to stay the hand of death and prolong my dad's life. Dad was 12 years older than Mom and always stated that Mom would out live him and advised us that when his time came she would lack nothing. After the dream I called my son, Trent, to ask him to help me pray. Before I could ask, Trent said, "Mom, I have a feeling about death. I believe Granddad is about to leave and go to heaven." In fact it was a year of much death. Three young people at our church, ages 18, 15 and 9, all died unexpectedly. Also, a close friend of mine, Hazel Jones, lost her battle to cancer in November. To say the least, that year felt like a whirlwind of sorrow. But in the midst of this pain, I had the joy of experiencing the birth of my second precious granddaughter, Amaya Sabrina Dawn, born November 28th. She was given the name Sabrina in honor of my younger sister Sabrina who passed at 21 years old some years earlier.

I was scheduled to attend a conference in California that November. Ironically, my parents' church anniversary was during that same week I was visiting. Due to unforeseen circumstances, the guest pastor who was scheduled to speak during the final service was not able to attend. The chairman of the Anniversary Committee requested of my dad that I minister the closing sermon. I was honored to do so but yet I had an unusual feeling during the service that I could not explain? A fond memory of that service was when Dad stood before the congregation and expressed his love for Mom, telling her how special she was to him. I now know that God orchestrated the timing of my being in California to witness that very special moment.

In a few weeks Mom was scheduled to come to Ohio to visit me and my family. Around that same time my husband was scheduled to leave on an African mission trip the second week of December. Mom was excited to visit and looking forward to meeting her newest great-granddaughter with the middle name of her beloved daughter, Sabrina. I could hardly wait! My taste buds were ready for Mom's greens and peach cobbler. Prior to my husband's departure for Africa, we went out to dinner at our favorite restaurant in Cincinnati. Mom was scheduled to arrive that evening. I had made prior arrangements with my son-in-law, Doug, to pick Mom up from the airport in Dayton. However, he called us while we were at the restaurant to advise that Mom's plane had been delayed in Chicago and re-routed to arrive at the Cincinnati Airport. When Doug met Mom at the airport he noticed that she did not look or seem herself and became concerned. We headed home to meet them. In the meantime I called my friend, Minister Jean Harvey, a pastor's wife and former nurse, and asked if she would go over and assess Mom's condition at the house prior to our arrival. Mom expressed that she had weakness on her right side. We called our physician, Dr. Morris Brown, and advised him of her symptoms. He admitted her into the hospital. Subsequently, it was determined that Mom had had a stroke while traveling on the airplane. I couldn't believe it! Her sister Daisy, who was in her late 60's, had also had a stroke on an airplane in November of the prior year which led to her death. This was unbelievable! Mom's initial prognosis was optimistic, (coupled with lots of prayer, of course). I learned the true meaning of: **Proverbs 3:5-6**: *"Trust in the Lord with all of your heart...."* (KJV)

I thought my mom would fully recover; however, on January 15, there was an unexpected change in her status and Mom went home to be with the Lord. "God, I did not see this coming!" As I stated in chapter 1, at that time I felt like God had let me down. The vision my sister saw in September of a coffin at the door had been a premonition of Mom's death. Although my sister refused to accept it at the time, it was in fact Mom.

I recalled a time when I was attending a funeral at H.H. Roberts Funeral Home in Dayton when I suddenly heard in my mind, "When your mom dies, bring her here." Well, of course, I quickly brushed away and refused to accept any thought of that from my mind. However, the following Monday after Mom's death, I did just that and called the funeral home. The funeral home personnel was gracious and made arrangements quickly. Mom had brought with her a beautiful gray suit, ranch mink hat and accessories. It was almost as if she had planned it. We held one Homegoing Service at our church, Maranatha Worship Centre, in Dayton, Ohio, on that Wednesday evening. It was followed by a second and final Homegoing Service at my parents' church, St. Paul Church of God in Christ in Bakersfield, California.

On the plane ride accompanying Mom's body back home to California, I saw a vision of Mom in Heaven embracing my 21 year old sister, Sabrina, who died unexpectedly several years prior. This vision brought me peace and joy. I could hear Sabrina calling out to her, "Mommy!" Although, it didn't surface in my mind again until she passed, the dark gray coffin with the beautiful red roses I saw in November, represented Mom, not Dad. I referred to my mom as "My Rose" and I wrote this poem about her several years earlier.

"My Rose"

My Rose is a special rose to me,
you can't find her everywhere.
Her warmth, soft glow,
and beauty aren't easy to compare.
If My Rose was in a contest,
the judges couldn't rate her fair,
Because the chemistry of My Special Rose
is really unusually rare.
There's one mentioned in Proverbs 31,
but it's a very expensive price,
I'm glad I already have My Rose;
now I won't have to sacrifice.
Most flowers bloom in the springtime,
or a certain time of year,
But whenever I need her cheer or comfort,
My Rose is always near.
My Rose has been hurt so many
times by people who tried to misuse her,
The special part about My Rose is no one could
permanently bruise her.
God never forgets a beautiful rose for
He's the one who made them,
and My Loving Rose gets very special care
because she always praises Him.
She lifts her face of petal and smiles
as she greets God's morning dew,
She lifts those leaves of praise towards Heaven,
and tells Jesus, "I Love You!"
When I was but a tiny babe,
My Rose, she cared for me,

And held me in her loving arms,
and stroked me tenderly.
As I grew up her little child,
she steered me in the right way,
And knowing things I would face in life,
she taught me how to pray.
I know by now you've guessed My Rose,
and I'm not trying to cover,
This beautiful, soft, and tender Rose is,
My Sweet and Loving Mother.

The Unseen and The Unknown

I Corinthians 13:9 (KJV) tells us, "For we know in part, and we prophesy in part." The God's Word Translation (GW) of I Corinthians 13:9-10 reads, "Our knowledge is incomplete, and our ability to speak what God has revealed is incomplete. But when what is complete comes, then what is incomplete will no longer be used."

Do we always see things as they are? When we have premonitions or see things they are not always explicit. They can be symbolic or the reverse of what we see. I am sure in many instances that dreams, visions and premonitions turn out to be just as they were revealed. However, I don't care how profound and devout we are spiritually or naturally, we can never solely rely on our own powers and abilities.

I recall a young lady I met when I was pregnant

with my first child. I really wanted a girl but back then ultrasounds were not readily used for gender determination. This young lady advised me that her mother was an "Expert", a "Prophet", and could determine the gender of a baby. This young lady already had a son and her mom told her that she was having a girl this time, so she proceeded to pick colors and buy things that would be appropriate for a baby girl. My husband wanted a boy and he had a dream that he was holding a baby girl over his shoulder. Because we took a dream "as a dream" (since there was a 50:50 chance it could be right or wrong),). I bought yellow and neutral colors for my baby. One month later when I delivered, I had my beautiful baby girl! This young lady congratulated me and we waited for the arrival of her "daughter" one month later. It turned out that we welcomed her "bouncing baby boy!" - LOL!

During one of my earlier ministry experiences, I had an eye-opening revelation. My husband had a dream where he said he saw one of our ministry leaders, Sister Betty Matthews, (who was not even 55 years old and appeared to be in good health), in a pink and silver coffin. He said, "We have to pray and call others to pray."

I went to a church women's meeting a couple of days later. Sister Matthews who was married with children and grandchildren was not present at the meeting but we prayed about this situation. We did not reveal who the person was but we decreed and declared that the plans of the enemy would be destroyed.

I had to leave town the next week so I tried to visit Sister Matthews before I departed. I had been to her house many times before but on this occasion I could not find her house! I went up and down the street to no avail. I was running out of time before having to head back and pick up my kids from school. I had to move on but I left bewildered. After being in California for a week, my husband called to tell me that Sister Matthews went to the doctor's office with "flu-like" symptoms, aspirated, and was rushed to ICU. Upon my return home our women's leader, Sister Lenoir, and I went to the hospital. Sister Matthews could not speak due to having a breathing tube. We made repeated visits to the hospital; however; we began to notice that Sister Matthews did not appear as if she wanted to continue to "fight" to stay in this world. (But I understood later).

I now understand that man has a will. If man gets a glimpse of Glory, is tired of pain, life's drama, unknown trials, etc., and ready to be with God, then the person has the final say. My husband stated after being disappointed and spending much time in prayer that our "warring" was not for Sister Betty Matthews, but instead for her family to remain committed to Christ and not lose their faith.

One of my dearest friends, Marshelle, was a beautiful woman inside and out. We referred to each other as, "my sister from another mother." Marshelle was younger than 50 years old when she went to be with Jesus following complications from what was considered a minor surgery. I felt that her time to leave us was way too soon.

Marshelle had premonitions. She would say little things from time to time such as, "If something were to happen to me, I know that David, (her devoted husband), would take care of things, but could you look after our daughters if something were to happen to us both?" I couldn't believe what I was hearing, I said, "Oh, Girl, you're not going anywhere, we're not even going to talk about that." Looking back I noticed she had said it several more times until I reluctantly said, "Yes", to caring for her daughters should something happen to her and her husband. David later told me that a few months prior to her passing she had said to him, "David, I won't be here long." His adamant response was, "Who is going to help me with these girls?" Sarcastically, Marshelle said, "You've got this, David; they listen to you better than me, anyway." Marshelle definitely knew something that we didn't know.

After her transition, a letter of advice and instruction for her two daughters was discovered in a Bible she left at home, she had told me in the event of her death to see that they received these letters. We now live in the house she had foretold me about before her death.

I prayed from the bottom of my soul for Marshelle's healing. I cried, "God, I love her, Lord! Please! This is my sister!" Marshelle had been a true friend and my support system. She had helped me with my kids and when it came to decorating for events she was exceptionally gifted. I could count on Marshelle to see that things were carried out to the maximum. She was a true friend, without an agenda who was right there when I needed her. Those friends are not always easy to find and life teaches you to cherish those friendships.

Although, Marshelle's loss was unexplainable and painful I still saw the hand of God. Three nights before Marshelle made her departure I dreamed that she was in her hospital bed but sat up and gave me a big smile. She was in beautiful white attire. I just knew that she was healed! In the dream she was no longer on a respirator, did not have a tracheotomy, nor an IV. However, later it became clear to me that it did not mean she would be healed in this world, but complete and whole in her transformed body.

David called me to advise that they were headed to the hospital due to Marshelle having an irregular heartbeat. Her breathing was shallow. Marshelle fought hard. David, their daughters, and other relatives were around her bed. We prayed. We cried. I begged God to work a miracle. She continued to fight. After a while I allowed God to speak to my heart. I asked her youngest daughter, Danesha, "What is your Mom saying to you?" She replied, "She says she's tired." Her husband was grieving and could not bear to see the love of his life in this condition. Suddenly, I had a revelation unlike any other before: "The birth into this world is a process that can't be rushed. The birth into the next world is also a process that can't be rushed." In the midst of pain is the beauty of new life. In the natural mind it may seem like an oxymoron but Psalms 116:15 reads, "Precious in the sight of the Lord, is the death of his saints." (KJV)

I walked over to Marshelle to get as close as I could and felt her spirit pulling on me. I said, "Marshelle. What is it? What do you want me to do?" I could hear in my spirit that she was worried about her two daughters' salvation. Therefore, I gathered the family members around and led her daughters and all those willing to recommit themselves to Christ in "The Sinners' Prayer".

Immediately after the prayer the monitor made a beeping sound and Marshelle stepped into Eternity. The medical team said they had never seen such a glorious departure.

Another glorious departure was my dad's who went home to be with Jesus four and a half years after Mom. The way in which he departed brought peace and comfort to us. We could not have asked for a sweeter goodbye in the face of sorrow. A couple weeks prior to Dad's departure, he had a dream. Dad's dreams and visions were something common to hear when I was growing up. He shared with my sister, Darl, that he saw himself sitting in the second pew of his church instead of taking his normal position in the pulpit. There was a beautiful woman coming down the aisle behind him. He had never seen a woman so beautiful and he fell in love with her. She was in all white and singing a song, "I love Him, I love Him, because He first loved me, and purchased my salvation on Calvary...." Dad said he got up and left with the woman. Darl asked him, "Dad, who used to sing that song in a high soprano voice?" He exclaimed, "Your mother! That was your mother singing!"

One month later, on August 18th, Dad went to evening service at his church. My cousin, Stephanie, was assisting him that evening. He decided to sit on the second row in the center of the sanctuary where he could minister to the congregation. His subject that night was "Rest in the Lord" (I Thess. 4:13) (KJV): "But, I would not have you to be ignorant, brethren, concerning them which are asleep, that ye sorrow not, even as others which have no hope." Upon completing his sermon, ironically, he did not take up an offering. He gave direction and instructions to his flock, then closed the service with Benediction Prayer and Goodbye Greetings. Those present stated that Dad glanced back over his right shoulder and then fell forward. He was taken to Memorial Hospital where all the natural resuscitation interventions were attempted. When I was called in Dayton, I knew in my spirit that my Dad had been escorted by my Mom from his earthly house to their heavenly mansion.

CHAPTER 4

Supernatural CAUTION! Signs

Dad had spoken a lot about his father, whom, I never met. My grandfather was killed in an accident before I was born. Dad was the oldest boy of 12 children born to Cora and West. West had three older sons he brought into the marriage from previous relationships. Therefore, the house was comprised of 15 children and two adults. I can only imagine. The family sharecropped and farmed for their livelihood.

Dad told us that he was born in Forney, Texas, but the family moved to Fort Worth, Texas, where they lived during his upbringing. When he was in his late teens or early twenties he moved to Dallas, Texas and worked in a packing house. He sent money back home to help support the family. His older half-brothers had moved away from the area to begin their lives.

My grandfather, "Papa", was a devout church deacon who would walk several times a week to church with his wife and children for services. One summer night after service concluded the family began to walk home. Papa was a short distance ahead of the family when suddenly they heard the screeching wheels of a car, then a loud thud! A car filled with white teenagers hit Papa. Granny and the children ran up the road and found Papa's body lying in a pool of blood. It was a life-changing tragedy for the entire family. Papa was hit and run over by a 14-year-old boy that had taken his parents' car for a "joyride". Unfortunately, there was no "joy" for my Dad's family in this tragic occurrence. Subsequently, the Caucasian young man was only given a "slap on the wrist" with no real consequences.

When Dad's siblings came to Dallas and told him of their father's tragic demise, he then knew it was now his responsibility to take care of his Mom and siblings. Dad's formal education ended after the eighth grade due to family demands. However, he was ambitious and became a self-taught carpenter and business owner. He built several churches, houses, and schools while I was growing up. Despite his limited education, it did not stop him from assisting me in an Industrial Math course when I was in college.

Dad's family members shared that in his youth he was an up and coming boxer that was classified as a "knock out" fighter! I could go on and on about my dad aka "My Super Guy". (See: "My Super Guy" poem at chapter's end). In spite of my grandfather's accident and the difficulties that followed, my Dad's life took a turn for the better. He met an older woman named Mother Tiny Griffin who led him to Christ. Instead of giving guys a knock-out-punch, he decided to give Satan, who took the life of his father, a knock-out-punch!

Dad was now Deacon Nathaniel Duffey. He moved to Bakersfield, California and with the exception of two siblings, moved his family out West. My dad's younger brother, W.D., became the first preacher in the family. They called him "Little Boy Preacher". My dad proudly took him around so he could share the Gospel of Christ. Later, three more sons, including my father, became ministers of the Gospel.

I did not have the pleasure of meeting my grandfather but apparently he was a seer or had premonitions. My father shared something later in life that was mystifying to me. There were gruesome details to the death of his father. When the family arrived at the scene of the accident they found Papa in a pool of blood with one leg above his head and the other dismembered body parts. My dad felt his mother was never really quite the same after the accident. He shared that before leaving home

Papa told him, "I will die and it's going to be quick and sudden. I won't linger. It may look bad but I'll be okay." Papa had shared this hours before his accident and although Dad's heart was filled with pain, the conversation brought him peace, shalom.

Although my dad no longer had his father's words of wisdom in the natural, he continued to hear from Papa through dreams and visions, especially when he was about to make wrong life decisions. There is not enough time here to tell you about the times when my dad did not heed the warnings in dreams. These were not bizarre or crazy things that would cause you to be frightened, but he experienced unnecessary hardships as a result or not heeding to the warnings.

In Dad's "heyday", with Mom by his side, he was a spiritual force to be reckoned with. I have seen my dad (through God), work miracles. People would feel the power of the Holy Ghost and fall to the floor. He was referred to as a "demon buster"! I remember my dad sharing with me the night before the 9-11 Tragedy that he heard hundreds of death bells ringing in his ears.

The last two years of my dad's life were difficult and lonely. Young women were out looking for a "Sugar Daddy" and older gold digging women wanted to set their hooks into this old man for what he had; property; a nice car; a good church;

and a few nickels they hoped would make their lives easier. My sister, Darl, the grandchildren, prayer warriors, and me, were all on our knees consistently to keep these women away. I tried to remain spiritual but on a few occasions, I must admit, I wandered into the natural realm because those good sisters were working my nerves! We often underestimate the enemy who does not give up, nor sleep. He tries to take us down in our weakest state, but like Sampson, God will allow us to rise up from our blinded state to wreak havoc on the enemy's territory. In fact, there was a woman that lived in another state, (I'll refer to her as "Delilah"), who planned to make a move on my dad in his weakest state, but God said, "Enough is Enough"! The night before he transitioned Dad told my sister he dreamed he was running and a fierce lion was behind him and almost consumed him. Then he saw his Papa in a chariot. He rode up beside him, grabbed him by his clothing, and pulled himself into the chariot just before the lion consumed him, and they rode away. Thank God for Heavenly interventions and Supernatural CAUTION! Signs!

I will be the first to admit, I am not a frequent dreamer, nor do I have the vivid dreams and visitations that my sister experiences. But whenever it's a God encounter, I know the difference. After

Mom's homegoing, I had an unexpected visit that I will never forget. Without that visitation, I am not sure that my granddaughter, Amaya, would still be with us. A couple days after Mom's funeral, we were all in California at my parents' home. I told my daughter, Tranisha, and son-in-law, Doug, to go on to a hotel and I would watch the kids. Things were so stressful for all of us and I just wanted to give them a break. My grandchildren, Xaivera, 4, Brennan, 22 months, and Amaya, just seven weeks old, stayed with me. I placed the older children on the couch in the den outside my room and Amaya on the side of my bed in her infant carrier. While sleeping I had a dream. My mom came to the room and stood at the door. In this dream I knew Mom was gone and I began to tell her how much I missed her and just wanted to hug her. I followed her as she backed out of the room and headed toward the door where Dad was asleep. Suddenly, the dream transitioned and I heard suitcases on the right side of the bed moving. That was odd because they were too heavy to have moved on their own and neither the A/C unit nor the wind could have caused the movement. Then I heard Mom's voice telling me to look at Amaya. When I did the baby was covered with mucus and unable to make a sound! Mom said gently, "Pick her up, turn her over, and pat her back." Her calm voice kept me from panicking and I followed her instructions. The baby began to catch her breath. My sister suddenly came from the back room, looked in on the other children, Xaivera and Brennan, before asking, "Is everything ok?" My sister told me that a voice woke her up telling her that something was wrong with one of the kids. I later shared the full story with her. **AGAIN, SAVED BY A SUPERNATURAL CAUTION SIGN!**

Super or Natural Beginnings?

My Mom's parents, "Big Mama" and "Big Daddy" as we called them, were a major part of our lives. Mom was very loving and devoted to her parents. They lived near us and were always a part of our ministry and spiritual development. In fact, Big Mama led me to salvation and I invited Christ into my life when I was about 12 years old. She ministered during a revival at my dad's newly-formed church in Bakersfield which was his second church. His primary church was a few miles away in a neighboring town.

Oddly enough, Mom and Big Mama were polar opposites. Big Mama was the "life of the party" and a powerful speaker. On the opposite end my mom, an impressive speaker and teacher in her own right, was quiet and like an "engine behind the train". She made sure that things ran smoothly.

Big Daddy was kind-hearted but firm. He was a devout deacon in my dad's first church and later became the pastor. Our denominational overseer sent my dad on an assignment to preach at a tent in an urban area of Earlimart, California. Initially there was just a handful of people but the congregation eventually grew large and a church was officially established. Dad built the building for the growing congregation which was named "House of Prayer" at my grandfather's recommendation. I'm sure 10 -12 years earlier while a deacon, Big Daddy never imagined that he would become the pastor of that church.

Big Daddy shared a story once that opened my eyes. God gave him an unexpected supernatural word of CAUTION! as a warning that perhaps saved his life. He saw a hitchhiker on the side of the road. Big Daddy thought to himself, "Why not?" He pulled over and waited for the man to run to the car and hop in. Just as the man caught up and reached for the door, Big Daddy said he heard a boisterous voice shout, "No!!!" He then pressed hard on the gas pedal and took off leaving the man behind. This behavior was out-of-character for Big Daddy. Later he heard that several people had been killed by an unidentified hitchhiker! Big Daddy had heeded the word of CAUTION, thank God!

A different kind of experience was witnessed when one of my dad's minister friends shared with him that he once picked up a man that later appeared as an angel resembling Bishop C.H. Mason, founder of the Church of God in Christ. He said he was riding in the back seat of his car and said, "Jesus is Coming Soon!", then disappeared. Thankfully, Dad's friend didn't have an accident.

Big Mama suffered a stroke in June, at age 70. Big Mama had gone to the Bay Area to visit her youngest two daughters Florence and Daisy. Mom and Uncle M.C. rushed to her side. Although the doctors did not give a positive report, Mom was optimistic that her mother would be healed and all would see a miracle. Big Daddy and her siblings were hopeful. Mom stood on unshakeable faith and relied on **Hebrews 11:1**: *"Now Faith is the substance of things hoped for, the evidence of things not seen."*

Despite our personal wishes, we have to seek God and ask, "What is your sovereign will" in this circumstance?" We also, must remember that the person has a free will which is a major part of the equation. We have all experienced a person who moved not in faith but presumption, and sometimes just plain old foolishness!

I was not able to go to California to see about my grandmother as I was pregnant, with my son, Trevon, and due in mid-July. Mom and Big Mama had planned to visit me when I delivered to help me with my other 2 children, Tranisha, 4, and Trenton, nearly 2. When I delivered, July 13, Mom was unable to come as Big Mama was still in a dire condition. Instead she sent my youngest sister, Sabrina, to Dayton to help me with my young children. Sabrina's hands were really full caring for two small children. It was a difficult time for both of us. I was young and use to having my Mom around especially during challenging times.

I clearly remember being in my basement putting clothes in the washer when I heard a voice say, "You can go home now." Then my sister, Darl, called to let me know that Big Mama had passed. My Mom was devastated, to say the least. She had been standing on her faith and going about her normal routine, such as canning peaches for herself and Big Mama. She had even taken a three day break and left the Bay Area hospital with plans to return. She then received the shocking phone call. Mom had remained steadfast that Big Mama would soon recover. When I called Mom she could not speak and only sobbed uncontrollably. I had never seen my mom like that.

Sabrina and I prepared ourselves and my children to fly home to California. We had our struggles enroute, especially at the Chicago airport. Trenton ran off! A man brought him back to me and said, "This little boy tried to go down the up escalator!" Looking back, I can't help but to think of the old song, "My Soul Looks Back and Wonders…How I Got Over!"

Big Mama's death was the first major loss for our family. With the help of God, we got through the planning and the funeral. Mom grieved heavily and we prayed for Mom's deep grief to subside. God answers in mysterious ways. One night Darl had a powerful vision that I could actually feel when she shared it with me. She said that she saw Big Mama standing in front of her. At first she appeared as a younger version of herself, smiling, then began to age in her appearance to the last time we saw her in good health prior to the stroke. Big Mama was unhappy and expressed her displeasure with Mom's long and hard grieving. Darl then saw Big Mama into the future but she was sitting in a wheelchair in a debilitating state. It appeared that she needed someone to fully take care of her. Big Mama then expressed that she did not want to live like this, existing from day-to-day. She said, "Tell your mother if she continues to grieve, I'll have to come get her!" She then changed back to her former appearance, then left. Darl said this was bizarre!

Initially, she was afraid and apprehensive about sharing this information with our mom. Finally she did share it, and to our surprise, Mom's attitude changed. She began to move out of the deep grief. It was difficult for Darl to share, but only God knew that it was the Supernatural Caution! sign Mom needed to start living again.

Presently, I counsel many experiencing grief. I attempt to alleviate the pressure of grief by sharing with the person that no one can tell you how to grieve. We may never fully get over the loss but we do have the God-given ability to adjust as time progresses. However, if deep grief lingers too long, and no progress is made within a reasonable amount of time, it can damage us emotionally and physically. I know Mom was disappointed and likely angry with God. If He chooses not to move in the way we want, or prayed, we must know that God is too wise to allow a mistake. **Romans 8:28** tells us, *"And we know that all things work together for good to them that love God, to them who are called according to his purpose."*

Many people say, "Don't question God!" However, many times we are not honest with ourselves. I say, "Why not question God?" His own son, Jesus, while on the cross asked, "Father, why has thou forsaken me?" Yes, we may get upset with God's decisions but he understands us and can handle it. I tell people in doing so just keep a noble level of respect when questioning God.

We must remind ourselves that death is an enemy and was not part of God's divine plan. Because of man's sin in The Garden (Genesis) death entered the equation. The enemy, Satan, comes to kill, steal, and destroy, but Christ came that we might have life more abundantly (John 10:10). Although death interrupted God's plan because of sin, God, in the person of Jesus Christ, intervened on our behalf. He came down and bought us back with the sacrifice of blood and gave us back eternal life in a place He prepared for us. So we and our loved ones have hope of everlasting life with a brand-new immortal body.

My Super Guy

There's nobody like my super guy,
He can climb the highest mountain
He can soar across the sky!

My friend said her's was real tough, too
But I quickly informed her
there was nothing my super guy couldn't do.

Why, he could swim the deepest ocean,
The fastest sprinter on dry land,
Why,he could even grab a lion and crush it,
with only one hand!

Now, this mighty super tough guy
Was much more than a fleeting fad.
Yup! This mighty super tough guy
was my super duper dad!

Well, I told those silly kids at school
How my dad could beat their dads to mush!
But then my mom heard me bragging, and said,
"Gal, you'd better hush!"

"But, mom, can't I tell them
that dad's uzi in the closet can blow
them off the map?
O.K. mom, I'll shut up.
Please don't embarrass me with a slap!

Mom, I know it's just a hunting gun.
So what, if all dad kills are rabbits?
But I thought that making his gun a lil' bit bigger,
Wasn't a real bad habit."

At the county fair, we would mount the biggest
coasters My dad wouldn't even bat an eye!
I clasped his hand and leaned on his arm,
and thought,
OOOH what a super guy!

Dad would grab the big hammer
And the whole crowd stood confound.
He'd grab it with all confidence,
Knowing he'd ring the bell each round.

On my wedding day,
he walked me down the aisle.
I felt happy, secure, loved and confident, As they
played "Here Comes the Bride," Knowing he
approved and was by my side.

As a P.K., I observed difficult circumstances.
I thought," Lord, how will my
mom and dad behave?"
Two things they never failed to show me
Was God' s mercy and they were saved.

I watched him treated unfairly by some
It would nearly break my heart.
He never would retaliate back,
but Trusted in God to protect his part.

Now older, Dad still mounts the pulpit.
He' s really quite an anointed preacher.
And always concerned about the people of God.
He's also a great counselor and teacher.

I found out that muscles didn't make my dad,
Nor was he hurt by his lack of education.

*But his love for God and family,as well as his
integrity Makes him a rarity in this nation.*

*Grown up, I realize that a super guy like dad,
Was more than mere fascination;
That he was what God designed a father to be,
From the beginning of creation.*

*He possessed those God-like qualities
Not just provision, guidance,
and discipline, but love.
Now I thank God I know I've been blessed By
only the heavenly father above*

*As an adult, I realize his super strength
Was far beyond what I could see.
It was the godly principles, morals,
integrity and love
Those super qualities Dad passed to me*

*Tribute to my dad Bishop Nathaniel Duffey Sr,
By: Dr. Bev Duffey-Martin Ph.D., D.Min*

CHAPTER 5

Visions of Comfort

Some experiences in our lives could be classified as a Category 5 hurricane with storms and winds exceeding 165 miles per hour! When I was told about the unexpected death of my youngest sister, Sabrina, at the young age of 21, I felt that I had been hit with such a hurricane. I am sure people can identify with such an untimely loss. It felt like the earth stood still. If you haven't felt such a catastrophic blow, then you are blessed. But my dad used to say, "Just keep on living."

Sabrina came to Ohio the year prior to stay with my family while she attended a local university in the area. She had gone home to California but was expected to return to Ohio in about a month to continue her studies. Her death devastated my parents, to say the least. However, Mom seemed to handle her grief more head-on this time when compared to the death of her mom as detailed in the previous chapter. Sabrina's death occurred just one year and eight months after Big Mama's passing.

Sabrina was delightful, humorous, and a great song leader and choir director. She was so full of life! Others would comment that she had wisdom, compassion, and leadership abilities far beyond her years. Sabrina made a statement several times (beginning as a teenager), that I didn't understand, "I won't live past age 21." Of course, we rebuked her every time for making this negative statement! A few days prior to her death, she asked Darl, "Can I do what really makes me feel happy?" Darl did not understand what she was saying, nor did Sabrina explain exactly what made her happy. I previously recall Sabrina making this statement several months prior to her death, "There's no house so beautiful, no marriage so perfect, and no kids so cute that I need any of it." Did she have a glimpse of Glory that made her so desire to be with and in the presence of God? Was her work here on earth finished? Some answers, I guess, we'll never know. I used to hear Big Mama say, "We'll understand it better by and by and further along we'll understand why?" In the meantime, we have to know that *"absent from the body is to be present with the Lord!"* **(2 Corinthians 5:8)**, where there is joy, peace and happiness.

The cause of Sabrina's death was inconclusive. A small blood clot was located; however, it was not deemed significant enough to be the cause of her death. When I last spoke to Sabrina, I called home on a Sunday night, two days prior to her passing. She was experiencing some flu-like symptoms, but we still had a great conversation. Sabrina had been resistant to go to the doctor but finally agreed to go on Tuesday. That morning after taking her bath, she lay down on our parents' bed and asked Mom to come read the Bible with her. Mom was busy and at first told her "Sabrina go ahead. You can read it for yourself." Shortly thereafter, Mom agreed to sit down to read with her. She then told Mom, "Satan has tried to tell me he's in control," and then smiled, "but I know the real winner is Jesus." Sabrina's favorite scripture was **Psalms 91**. Mom noticed Sabrina's lips moving, but she was making no audible sound. Mom asked her, "Sabrina, What are you saying?" Sabrina said, "Sshh! I'm talking to God." Sabrina was somewhat fidgety and apparently restless. She seemed a little faint and pale, so Mom tried to use cool towels on her face to revive her but she didn't want that. Mom called Big Daddy who lived nearby. As Mom tried to comfort her with cold compresses on her head Sabrina pushed Mom's hand away. Big Daddy sensed what was happening and convinced Mom to allow her to lie back on the bed undisturbed.

Dad came home just as the ambulance was leaving and rode with her to the hospital. As the family waited at the hospital staff eventually came out and advised that they had done everything they could but could not revive her.

My family could not reach me by phone so they called my husband at the dental office and shared the devastating news with him. When I stopped by the office in route to picking up our three children from the sitter I could tell something was on his mind but he didn't want to tell me then and there. He asked me to go home and said he would meet me there after finishing with his patients. I asked, "Is everything o.k.? Are the kids o.k.?" I then asked, "Is Sabrina ok?" He said, "Why did you ask that?", but avoided answering my question. I tried to think positive and assume he had a gift or some sort of surprise for me but when I arrived home nothing seemed different. When I saw that there was no gift or surprise I called my husband and asked, "What's going on?" I could sense and hear in his voice that there was a problem so I pressed him to tell me what he was withholding. He said, "I'll be home soon and will talk to you then." I said, "I can't stand this. Tell me the truth! What happened?" He finally answered, "Sabrina passed." I screamed, "WHAT!" I began shouting, "WHY? WHY?" and began hitting the wall.

Everything was a blur. I felt like I was mechanical and moving in slow motion.

As a friend, Sister Lenoir and her daughter, Eleanor, helped me pack to go to California, I called Mom. Surprisingly she could actually talk and tell me what happened which was nothing like her response to losing Big Mama. Her response gave me a bit of comfort. Nevertheless, it was a difficult time and I felt as if I were moving through a dark cloud, to say the least.

I boarded the plane with my 6 year old daughter, Tranisha, heading to California. It was the worst trip of my life! When I arrived in Bakersfield I could not even go home. I could not bear to see my family, the house and certainly not Sabrina's room. I was devastated, to say the least.

I was to have called the family to pick me up upon my arrival but not having the courage to go home, I just walked aimlessly in despair through town. At some point I heard the voice of God say, "I will not put more on you than you can bear." With an attitude I snapped back, "I can't bear this!" God gently said, "Switch gears." To which I responded, "How!" He informed me to switch gears from my earthly language to my heavenly language , but I was still questioning the purpose of that language. I could recall **I Corinthians 14:15** ***"What is it then? I will pray with the spirit, and I***

will also pray with the mind…" (That means the first is not understood by the natural mind.) At that point I was hurting so bad that I was willing to try anything. Finally, in desperation I tried it, and found that it was the key to my peace. Tranisha finally said, "Mommy, my legs hurt." It was dusk by then and I finally had the strength to call home. My family members had been looking for me and were getting worried since they hadn't heard from us. The Acts 2 power of God gave me the strength to handle everything and be with my family in our time of sorrow.

Sabrina looked like a beautiful bride. Her Homegoing Service reflected her life so well. Young people came to Christ and it was like a revival instead of a funeral! Sabrina's spirit witnessed to all those present.

The days following my sister's passing, my family really needed comforting. Mom wondered what more she could have done and Dad felt guilty about not being at the house sooner. In the midst of my own pain my other sister and brother needed comforting too. God spoke to my heart and said, "Beat grief up." It didn't make sense to me? He said, "Set your clock, wake up, get your parents up, and beat grief up before it controls your day." This was my assignment. The first morning was a weeping session but by the fifth morning, my dad began to gain strength, took the lead and said, "Yes, to the will of God!"

I stayed a few weeks with my parents. Darl and I cleaned out our sister's room and closet and helped Mom around the house. One day a card came in the mail from a woman named Evangelist Luckie. Evangelist Luckie had ministered during a revival at my dad's church a few months earlier. I had not met her personally but had heard good things about her through Sabrina and other family members. The card stated that she had an unusual experience and desired to share it with Mom. Darl and I had been shielding Mom from excessive phone calls and visits; however, I took it upon myself to call Evangelist Luckie. I told her that I was Sabrina's older sister and thanked her for the card. She warmly greeted me and was glad that she had received a response. Evangelist Luckie stated that she had never had an experience like this and was a little reluctant to share it with me but I assured her that it was o.k. She stated that she had been sitting at her organ in her home and praying earnestly for our family. When she looked up she saw Sabrina standing in the middle of the floor. The vision startled her but she stated that Sabrina was smiling and was pleasant and said, "Hi, Sister Luckie." She responded, "Hi, Sabrina." Sabrina advised her to tell our family that she did not want to come back because where she was there was such joy, happiness and peace. "They are going to miss me. Pray for them, and tell my friends whatever they do, don't miss Heaven and go to Hell. It's a terrible place!" Sabrina then walked past the room where Evangelist Luckie's daughters were sleeping, smiled, and disappeared.

Three days later, the evangelist said that Sabrina revisited her but was looking more serious that time. It was one week to the day that she had passed away. Sabrina asked her to fast on behalf of her Mom, Dad, sisters, and brother. Evangelist Luckie advised that Sabrina was wearing a speckled purple dress. Darl and I had seen that purple dress she described hanging in Sabrina's closet when going through her things. When I shared this message with Mom and Dad, Mom cried but it gave her a sense of peace and comfort.

I really had to pray and analyze this one. I knew that the message was not from Satan as he would have never told us not to go to Hell and give kudos to Heaven. Again, I was reminded that the Bible declares, *"absent from the body is to be present with the Lord!"* **(2 Corinthians 5:8)**, We have the privilege of joining the great cloud of witnesses. I am not privileged to know everyone's comfort story, but I know that many of my readers have stories that are yet untold.

I can recall one day having a brief signet of comfort that will always remain in my heart and in my mind's eye. We were young pastors with a new church. Our small church was located on Hoover Avenue in Dayton, Ohio. A delightful young man. Steve, (probably in his late teens), with a beautiful smile, stopped by our church. He started to attend our church regularly. His family, extended family, and friend, soon joined the church. Subsequently, Steve joined the military and we began seeing him less frequently except when he was home on leave. WOW! He was so handsome in his uniform.

One morning we got a call that Steve had been killed in a train accident. My husband and I rushed to be with the family. It was another devastating situation. As the family gathered and wept I remember Steve's dad looking up from his grief and saying something so memorable that I will never forget. "This is STILL the day the Lord has made. I will rejoice and be glad in it."

Steve's Homegoing Service was beautiful and truly celebrated his life. He had made quite an impression on his family and friends. Following the service we went to the V.A. Cemetery for his final disposition. As I stood next to a sister in Christ, I saw something amazing. A leaf lifted up from the ground and for some reason caught my eye. I thought it would just whirl around and fall to the ground again but it continued to go higher and higher until it was finally out of sight. I saw this as a sign that Steve had made it and was now apart of the Heavenly Host.

Another life-changing experience I vividly recall was while living in Los Angeles, California in my early twenties. In the midst of tragedy I still saw the love and comfort of God. I met many nice and caring people. One friend I met named Tralena had a sister, Vickie. They came from a large family. Vickie had 3 sons and a cute 2-year-old daughter. As we became closer friends, Tralena shared that Vickie and her husband, Dusty, had had some rough times. In fact, they were told by a couple of ministers, including their senior pastor, that it would not be in their best interest to marry one another. But they were "in love" and married anyway. We have all heard the cliché "love is blind." I say, one can also add "Marriage will open your eyes and put bi-focals on them!"

Things became really rocky for Vickie and Dusty after the birth of their second baby. Dusty had a reputation of being very violent toward Vickie. Afterward, he would cry, say he was sorry and then make empty promises. They stayed together but separated off and on until they had their fourth child, a desired daughter. In late August, they were separated which was typical for this type of relationship. Vickie was warned by an evangelist at a revival in Northern California, "Do not go back home and reconnect with your husband." However, after returning to L.A. her husband begged her, "Come home. Let's be a family again."

Shortly after the warning Vickie's teenage brother went to her house so that she could take him to their Mom's home as school was staring the next day. When Vickie went to the bathroom to take a quick bath she heard Dusty and her brother struggling. She heard her brother pleading, "Stop, Dusty. Stop!" She came out in a robe to find Dusty hitting her brother with a wrench. When she tried to stop him he began hitting her too. She ran up the street to get help. When she returned home with the police and a rescue squad her brother was unconscious. Before riding in the ambulance to the hospital with her brother, she instructed her children to stay in the house and that she would be back soon.

While being treated in the ER, police officers approached her and said to her, "We have bad news for you." She tearfully replied, "I know... my brother died." They confirmed this but then they told her that there was something more. She looked up at them with tears flowing and said, "My children are dead!" Dusty had snapped! He ran a tub full of water, drowned the four children, and invited the police officers inside afterward to take a look.

Words cannot express the overwhelming grief and the vision of seeing five coffins filled with young innocent lives. By now you are asking where is the comfort in this devastating story? A few days later, Vickie said she was lying in her bed lonely, sobbing and feeling the worst guilt and pain she had ever felt. Then she saw the hand of God take the ceiling of the room and rolled it back like a scroll. She could see into the "Supernatural Heavenlies"! She saw her brother and children all dressed in white filled with joy and peace. One of the little boys that use to always be into something was playing in a fountain. God allowed the vision to be open for an extended period of time. She described each one of them and what they were doing. When the time had come for the ceiling to close they said, "Bye, Mommy., Bye, Mommy. We will see you soon."

I learned three valuable lessons through Vickie's tragic experience. Lesson #1: I learned to listen and seek the face of God concerning all my relationships and stand on **Proverbs 3:6**: *"... in all your ways acknowledge Him, and He will direct your paths."* That means not going on feelings but instead asking God, "What are you saying?" Lesson #2: I learned to listen to those persons He puts into my life to give me wisdom regarding relationships, etc. If everyone else is seeing red and I'm seeing gold, stop...pray...and reconsider. And Lesson #3: I learned through this tragic experience that we serve a gracious, loving, and comforting Father.

Through stories of comfort I feel compelled to share two more recent heartfelt accounts.

Account #1:

Pastors Mike and Bonita Wilburn are precious Associate Pastors in our ministry. While writing this chapter I remembered the death of their son, LeeVon. On December 3, 2013,he was shot in the back and killed in his yard. It was a shocking tragedy! I had seen him come by the church about two weeks earlier. I will always remember his beautiful smile when he asked me about his mom before going into the sanctuary.

I spoke with Pastor Bonita about how God comforted her, her husband and the entire family through a message God sent by way of one of his younger brothers named Faith. Faith had sent a text message to another brother nicknamed, "Doc". Pastor Bonita stated, "I remember as plain as day the Sunday that our son, Faith, got a message from God that was for all of us concerning

LeeVon's death. Faith and all of my children, were questioning me and my husband as to why this tragedy happen to LeeVon? Why was he allowed to die like that? Shot in the back with none of us with him?" They said, "We know our parents love God. Why would God let this happen to LeeVon?" Our son, Faith, was at church in Columbus, Ohio, the next Sunday after LeeVon's death. The Pastor was talking about the Christmas Program. Faith said to himself, "I don't want to hear about this Christmas stuff. I'm getting up out of here!" However, Faith stated that out of the blue the pastor stated, "God knows your pain." Then God said in a whisper to Faith, and showed him an image of God sending one Angel down to breathe the breath of life into LeeVon, so that he could say, "JESUS!"

Faith's Comforting Word From God
(as sent to his brother via text message)

"Doc. God just whispered to me, 'The things I do is not for Man's understanding. Don't question me. I had to let the enemy come in and take LeeVon's physical life, so he would live eternally. LeeVon would have never come to the Lord while he was living. We had to lose life to gain life.' I believe that God sent down an angel to breathe life into him only for seconds so that he would realize he needed to call out the name of Jesus. See the devil's plan is to steal, kill, and destroy. The enemy started rejoicing because he thought he took another soul but God had another plan. As LeeVon lay there he was given time to call out Jesus' name. The angels began to rejoice and sing out praises because eternal life is better than this life on earth. The devil didn't see that coming and he was mad and Hell rumbled because the enemy had lost another soul. 'I am a forgiving God but every man and woman will be held accountable for the things they do in this life', God said. The things LeeVon did over his life caused him to lose his physical life but God knew what was best for him all along and allowed this. We can't understand why God would allow LeeVon to leave this earth the way he did because our motives are selfish. We wanted LeeVon here. God said, 'My thoughts are not your thoughts and my ways are not your ways. The heavens are higher than the earth and so are my thoughts and ways. You wanted LeeVon with you temporarily but now he reigns with me eternally!' Every Child of God has a testimony. LeeVon didn't get to give his testimony while he was living but he will have one through his death. His testimony is not to let your temporary life on earth run out before you receive your permanent life for eternity."

Account #2

Before sharing my final story of comfort I believe that on a daily basis we are protected by angels that watch over us and keep us from dangers seen and unseen. One day I was in Sam's Club looking for a Christian book to give to members of my youth dance team as birthday gifts. As I looked through the books I saw a Caucasian lady with beautiful white hair in my peripheral view. We made eye contact. She had a beautiful smile and we made conversation. I explained that I was looking for a good book that would be interesting for teens and hold their attention. The lady recommended Jesus Calling by Sarah Young. I began looking through the book And when I looked up to tell her "Thank You", she was nowhere to be found? I further thought, she didn't even have a shopping cart? My church youth love this book! I have lost count of the number of books now that I have given as gifts. I believe I had an angelic encounter!

My friend, Minister Jean Harvey, had a church member that was always helpful with whatever they needed him to do. He had a true servant's heart. He was married and had a 15-year-old daughter that adored him. She was a true "Daddy's Girl." Last year this gentleman had a heart attack and passed away unexpectantly. No one saw this coming. Several months following his death his daughter would cry non-stop at times as she missed her dad and friend terribly. One morning, she went into the bathroom to take a shower. As she exited the steamy shower she looked at the bathroom mirror. Written in the steam was a message in her dad's handwriting that read, "I love you!"

CHAPTER 6

What Does The Word Say?

Being aware of this controversial topic, I was initially reluctant to write this book. I am a person that prefers a homeostatic (stable) lifestyle...as Rodney King said, "Can't we just all get along?" When you have an assignment and you are not in charge of your own life, you are not truly happy until you follow the call of God. I am aware that many shut down when death experiences are mentioned. Why? First, because it is an uncomfortable subject. Secondly, there is a stigma attached regarding "ghosts, ghouls, and goblins." And thirdly, all that cannot be explained or understood is either ignored or will be attached to Satan.

Years ago, I knew that it could not be all attributed to Satan, but I could not explain it. An example was the visitation Evangelist Luckie received after my sister Sabrina's death and my friend Vickie's visitation following the deaths of her brother and four children along with other accounts that affirm that Heaven is the better place to spend eternity and that our spirits and souls never die. They remain alive forever. That's how we can embrace (Isaiah 61:3), which says, "He gives comfort to those that mourn and gives us the garment of praise for the spirit of heaviness." Regardless of what I think or feel, God's word is the final authority. It is the only book that details the past and goes beyond the present. You cannot exhaust this book. You can read it over and over and it still speaks to you with a new revelation. Some say that it contradicts itself, but they are trying to read it without God's revelation and knowledge. This reminds me of a book written in a foreign language but trying to use English concepts and interpretations.

I do not pretend to be a Biblical authority or theologian. I can only share with you what was revealed to me as I prayed, studied and asked God for his explanation. Three references in the Bible that I explored regarding life after death: I) The story of the Rich Man, **Luke 16:19-31**; II) The Great Cloud of Witnesses, **Hebrews 12:1**; and III) Jesus' journey into the heart of the Earth after His death: **Matt. 27:50-52**.

The Rich Man

The Story of the Rich Man has been referred to by some as a fictitious story, or a parable. But what differentiates it from being just a story or a parable is the fact that specific names and details are mentioned. It says in **Luke 16:19**, *"There was a certain rich man...clothed in purple and fine linen..."* In **Luke 16:19-31**: *"There was a beggar named Lazarus...filled with sores."* It also names Father Abraham, Lazarus, Moses, and the Prophets in this account. Jesus had not yet ascended; therefore, Lazarus was comforted in Abraham's bosom when the angels carried him there after he died. Abraham was holding him in his chest and consoling him because of his suffering in his lifetime. Abraham and the other patriarchs were still not in Heaven but in Sheol. When Hebrew Scriptures were translated into Greek around 200 BC the word Hades was substituted for Sheol. Sheol and Hades are the same place. There are three different terms in the Bible meaning for Hell: Sheol, Hades, and Gehenna. The difference between the three: Sheol/Hades - a non-permanent place or temporary address for those disembodied souls of the dead. In the **King James Version of the Bible**, grave is translated 31 times; "Hell" 31 times; "Gehenna" (aka: "The Lake of Fire"), 12 times; and "The Pit" 3 times. Sheol / Hades is where Jesus descended after death. There were two compartments where the departed awaited in a conscious realm. (See: **Matt. 5:22; 29-30; Matt. 10:28; Matt.18:9; Matt. 23:15, 33; Mark 9:43, 45, 47; Luke 12:5; and James 3:6**). More detail will be given in Jesus' Mission into the Heart of the Earth after Death. For an extensive view, there is a teaching by Theologian W. Edward Bedore Th.D., in his book: **Hell, Sheol, Hades Paradise and the Grave.**

Jesus himself in telling the story of The Rich Man and Lazarus describes Sheol / Hades as an abyss or gulf; a great space between them. The Upper Chamber was a place of hope for the conscious dead. The Lower Chamber was a place for the dead or lost. The certain Rich Man who was not named was tormented in the flames. He could see Lazarus and converse with Abraham and asked Abraham if Lazarus could dip his finger into water and cool his parched tongue? His second request was for Lazarus to return and warn his brothers not to come to that horrible place of torment. Abraham told him that they are given the same opportunity to change their ways of living as anyone else and if they refused to hear him they would end up suffering the same eternal fate.

The Cloud of Witnesses

I find comfort in the various translations of **Hebrews 12:1 (KJV)**, *"Wherefore seeing we also are compassed about with so great a cloud of witnesses, let us lay aside every weight, and the sin which doth so easily beset us, and let us run with patience the race that is set before us."* There are several other translations of that scripture that I would like to consider. **The New International Version (NIV)** says, *"Therefore, since we are surrounded by such a great cloud of witnesses, let us throw off everything that hinders and the sin that so easily entangles. And let us run with perseverance the race marked out for us."* In the **Amplified (AMP)** we see, *"Therefore, since we are surrounded by so great a cloud of witnesses [who by faith have testified to the truth of God's absolute faithfulness], stripping off every unnecessary weight and the sin which so easily and cleverly entangles us, let us run with endurance and active persistence the race that is set before us."* God's Word (GW) says, *"Since we are surrounded by so many examples [of faith], we must get rid of everything that slows us down, especially sin that distracts us. We must run the race that lies ahead of us and never give up."* This is the Message Bible (MSG) translation, "Do you see what this means – all these pioneers who blazed the way, all these veterans cheering us on? It means we'd better get on with it. Strip down, start running – and never quit! No extra spiritual fat, no parasitic sins. Keep your eyes on Jesus, who both began and finished this race we're in... "Also **Revelation 7:9** states, *"I am confident that our soul and spirit does not die, but remains alive. Join the great cloud of witnesses in the spiritual hall of fame."* **James 6:25** confirms that the body without the spirit is dead; therefore, the spirit does not die, but lives on eternally.

I have had the opportunity to speak with Dr. Prince Parker, a theologian and author of several books. He is a seminary professor in Spain and has had the privilege to travel the world. I shared my beliefs with him regarding the spirit and soul that never dies. Dr. Parker concurred with me and had a wealth of knowledge on this subject, He shared, "Our soul and spirit man are designed by the Creator to live forever. Because Man sinned in the Garden we lost our unlimited lifespan." There are scriptures that support these findings: **Hebrews 9:27 (KJV)**, *"And as it is appointed unto men once to die, but after this the judgment."* and **Romans 6:23**, *"For the wages of sin is death, but the gift of God is eternal life through Jesus Christ, Our Lord."*

I wondered how long Adam actually lived? After he sinned he lived 900 plus years before he died. Adam would have been eternal. Even though Man sinned, we are given a second chance according to **I Corinthians 15:52** which let's us know that we will be changed in a moment, in the twinkling of an eye., Our bodies will change from mortal to immortal. Our soul and spirit man will join the body and we'll be with Jesus forever! We serve such an awesome God! Although, Man sinned, Jesus Christ, who was second of the Godhead, volunteered as the Son of God to die and shed His blood in our stead. Yes, he was 100% GOD, but put on the robe of flesh and became 100% man. Jesus was touched with our infirmities; therefore, he could relate to our physical and emotional pain, lack, hurt, disappointment, betrayal, rejection, denial, etc. Everything we will or could ever suffer, Christ carried them to The Cross. Jesus allowed Man to beat him, spit in his face, put him on a cross and publicly shame him. Time will not permit me to give the gruesome details of his senseless crucifixion, but after his death he went into Hades and released those that were held captive. Jesus did all of this because *He loves you and me!* *HALLELUJAH!*

Jesus' Mission Into the Heart of the Earth After Death
Ephesians 4:8-10; I Peter 3:18-20; I Peter 4:6

We see Jesus praying in the Garden of Gethsemane outside the wall of Jerusalem. The wine or olive press is familiar in scripture. Olive oil depicts the anointing. There was a huge stone inside of a heavy circular stone where the olives were crushed. This represented that Jesus was anguished and was crushed. The main focus wasn't the physical death but the journey to set captives free that had died and gone to Sheol / Hades. Jesus knew he could have called a legion of 72,000 angels to set him free upon his request but he had a mission.

No one, including the patriarchs, was in Heaven as of yet. That's why the Rich Man could see Lazarus in Abraham's bosom. Instead, they were, in Hades which consisted of two compartments of the dead and the wicked dead. There was an abyss or gulf in between the two places. Jesus had to go into those compartments and preach to those imprisoned. Because this was not an easy task, he wanted the cup, as stated in **Hebrews 5:7**, to pass. He said, *"Father let this cup pass from me."* This word comes from the Greek word "EK" or "EX" - out of the place of death. Jesus did not want to be left there as no one had ever gone to Hades and returned. He kept asking the disciples to pray with him; lest they fall into temptation. Perhaps, you're wondering like me what the temptation was. The temptation was not to fight or flight, like Peter did, but instead to follow the will of the Father. Jesus was obedient despite knowing his fate and said, "Nevertheless, not my will, but thy will be done." In submission he gave the disciples permission to sleep on and get their rest. He not only submitted, but was prepared.

1. The Physical Death of Christ: Matt 20:50-51; Mark 15:37-38; Luke 23:44-46

Customarily, criminals were tied on a cross, but Jesus, a non-criminal, was nailed to The Cross and mocked. Some theologians say they considered using his elbow and shoulder when his hand split but instead his hands were nailed between the two bones of the forearm below the wrist. His feet were not positioned on a little platform as often pictured, but on that splintered cross and he had to lift himself upward enough to catch his breath. Jesus was beaten beyond recognition. They were not considerate. His face was not spared. Not only did he suffer from the crown of thorns but also of 39 lashes from a "cat of nine tails"! Christ suffered a horrible death!

Dr. Parker and other theologians concur that he died from asphyxiation. Crucifixion also put an added strain on the heart. After Jesus died they pierced him in the side to make sure he was dead. The veil of The Temple was rent but Jesus was already dead according to scripture. In Jewish custom they were not allowed to have the dead hang after sundown. Out from his body flowed blood and water. Most theologians maintain that he was dead approximately 1-2 hours. When they took Jesus off The Cross and placed his body in the tomb, his soul and spirit had already descended into Hades to preach to all those imprisoned.

2. Jesus Preached to the Imprisoned Spirits:
1 Peter 3:18-20; 1 Peter 4:6; Ephesians 4:8-10

Christ was put to death in the flesh but was quickened to eternal life in the spirit. When Christ went to preach to the imprisoned spirits he had to preach to everyone because all were born into sin. No one could come into the presence of God without Christ. This included those who were in the chamber of the dead; the righteous dead, and the evil dead who were unrighteous. Romans 3:23 tells us, "For all have sinned, and come short of the Glory of God." Those that died before The Flood, were large in number and Christ also preached to them.

Now due to Christ's finished work on The Cross we are redeemed from the curse of the law and are given multiple opportunities for forgiveness and redemption. Not just religion, which is man's effort to find God, but Christ extends Himself to us in the form of salvation. As an act of mercy Jesus went to those who had previously rejected him, such as those lost in The Flood and Sodom and Gomorrah, and admonished them to repent, receive Him, and be saved! Jesus had many references regarding the damnable acts of the men of Sodom and Gomorrah which include **Matt. 10:15, Matt 11:23-24; and 2 Peter 2:3-10**. This also lets us know in **Romans: 5:20**, *"Where sin abounded, grace did much more abound."* It also verifies that those acts committed are sin and sin cannot glory in his sight. Thank God, Man has a choice! Good and evil are set before us. We can choose to follow the flesh and what feels good. We can talk to ourselves or listen to others to justify sin. We can also take up our cross, follow Christ and be led to righteousness, peace and eternal life.

3. Jesus Comes Out of The Tomb: John 20:11-17

Jesus appears to Mary of Bethany, the younger sister of Lazarus and Martha, whose parents were deceased. Although Mary was close to him she did not recognize him after his crucifixion because He now appeared unto her in his glorified body. She was weeping and asked, "Where could they have taken, My Lord?", when Jesus called her by name. When she finally recognized Him she cried, "Rabboni!," meaning Master. He was no longer disfigured and bloodied as he was after his crucifixion. Jesus instructed her not to touch him as he had not yet ascended to the Father. The Father was to receive first fruits of his Resurrection. He told her to tell the brethren that He was ascending to the Father, and your Father, to My God, and to Your God.

Simultaneously, when Jesus appeared to Mary, He let those that believed and received him out of Hades and they were seen walking the streets. When the earth quaked following Jesus' crucifixion their bodies came up out of the ground. Prior to taking them to the Father, **Matt. 27:46-50** it speaks of how people in Jerusalem appeared alongside Jesus prior to going with Him to the throne of the Father. Graves were opened and many bodies of the Saints which slept arose.

4. Jesus Presented Souls to the Father: Hebrews 21:13

"Behold I and the children whom God has given me", were the first to go to Heaven. I would classify them as Pre-Rapture. Jesus presented these souls to the Father. I noticed that he always refers to us as "His children." Never, "my adults," or "senior citizens." But the endearing love that our Lord shows us is beyond our earthly imagination. He is not willing that anyone should perish. *"For God so loved the world that he gave his only begotten Son."*, **John 3:16**. All we have to do is believe, (which is proven by our actions), and in exchange He will give us everlasting life!

5. Jesus Returns to Earth: Luke 24:39; John 20: 24-28; 1 John 1:1

Jesus, after presenting himself and the captives to God, the Father, returned to Earth to communicate with those he mentored and loved. Jesus spoke with them and allowed them to touch Him as some were frightened and feared that he was a spirit. **Luke 24:39** say *"Behold, my hands and my feet, that it is I myself: handle me, and see; for a spirit hath not flesh and bones, as ye see me have."* Recall in Section 3) that Jesus would not allow Mary to touch Him prior to His ascending to the Father. **John 20:24-28** let's us know that after His return He allowed "Doubting" Thomas to touch Him. Jesus said to Thomas, "…reach your finger here and behold my hands; and reach your hand here and thrust it into my side; and do not be unbelieving, but believing." And Thomas answered and said to Him, "My Lord and my God!" Although, they could touch Jesus, He could supernaturally appear through closed doors according to **John 20:26**. They were witnesses to the Word of God that had been seen and heard being fulfilled. I **John 1:1 (KJV)** says, *"That which was from the beginning, which we have heard, which we have seen with our eyes, which we have looked upon, and our hands have handled, of the Word of life."*

6. Jesus Returns Back to The Father: John 7:33; John 18:28; John 20:17; John 14:2; John 14:12; Mark 16:19; Luke 24:51; Acts 1:9

Therefore, he said, "For a little while longer I am with you, then I go to him who sent me." Jesus' return to the Father was predicted in **Leviticus 16:15**. It was symbolic and spoke of the Mercy Seat. Also in **Psalms 68:18 (NASB)** it says, "You have ascended on high, you have led captive your captives; You have received gifts among men, even among the rebellious also, that the Lord God may dwell there." And **Luke 24:26 (NASB)** states, *"Was it not necessary for the Christ to suffer these things and to enter into His glory?"* We now know why it was so necessary.

In conversing with Dr. Parker, he made a profound statement, "If Man could have gone to Heaven without Christ's resurrection from the dead it would not have been necessary for Him to die on The Cross and pay the price for our sins." No one that died before Him had ascended. They were not with God or in the presence of God. They were not in Heaven, but in Hades. Remember, God's original plan in the Garden was that Man would live forever but sin changed the course. Adam and Eve, all of the patriarchs, and even John the Baptist who was considered the greatest of all Prophets, were in the realm of the dead in Hades. Even the smallest person is greater than John the Baptist because he died before The Cross and he did not experience the new birth and the Hope of eternal life.

We now have access and can go right into the presence of God. **Ephesians 1: 20-21 (NIV)** says, *"He exerted when he raised Christ from the dead and seated him at his right hand in the heavenly realms far above the rule and authority, power and dominion, and every name that is invoked, not only in the present age but also in the one to come."*

7. Jesus Sends A Comforter, The Holy Spirit
Pre-Comforter Scriptures: Luke 24:51; Mark 16:19
Comforter Scriptures: John 14:16, 26; John 15:26; John 16:7, 8, 13

We can see what took place in **Acts 1:9 (KJV)**, "And when he had spoken these things, while they beheld, he was taken up; and a cloud received him out of sight." In the Greek, The Comforter is referred to as Paraketos and convicts the world of sin. The third person of the Godhead, is The Holy Spirit. **John 14:16 (KJV)** declares: "And I will pray the Father, and he shall give you another Comforter, that he may abide with you for ever." Scripture identifies the characteristics and attributes of the Holy Spirit. Not only is He a Helper, but he will bring all things to our remembrance; all things that He has told us. Jesus said, "The Holy Spirit will also speak and testify about me.", **John 16:8**. *"...He will convict the world concerning sin, righteousness and judgment."* Jesus promised not to leave us comfortless. The Comforter will empower us to do the work of Christ. **Acts 1:8 (KJV)** says, *"But ye shall receive power, after that the Holy Ghost is come upon you: and ye shall be witnesses unto me both in Jerusalem (which represents Home), and in all Judea, and in Samaria (our Surroundings), and unto the uttermost part of the earth (Abroad)."* We were promised in **John 14:12 (KJV)** that ..."*Greater Works shall we do.*" Not only in quality, but also in quantity due to transportation, technology, etc., we can now reach the entire world in moments. I am grateful for the Word of God for it tells us in **Psalm 119:105 (KJV)** that *"Thy Word is a lamp unto my feet, and light unto our path."* This light exceeds far beyond what we have seen or can see.

CHAPTER 7

Transitioning From Fear To Faith

Most of us have heard the saying, "Everyone wants to go to Heaven, but no one wants to die." We believe in the "Heavenly Hope", but none of us are homesick. Why not? There is a fear attached to the unknown. How can we face and conquer the fear? Unless Christ delays his coming we must all die. My dad would often say, "Death. You never get use to it, because it always comes for someone different. But it's fair. No matter if you're rich, poor, black, or white. It does not discriminate...no one is exempt." Even though **Hebrews 9:27** reads *"And as it is appointed unto men once to die, but after this the judgment."* Life is choice-driven. Lifestyle can dictate early departure. Our bodies are like vehicles. If we don't do the proper maintenance the vehicle will not serve us well and ultimately stop running. Our lifetime can be altered by lifestyles and decisions. Although nothing catches God by surprise he knows our end from our beginning. But Man is a free moral agent. We can *"Choose you this day whom ye will serve,"* **Joshua 24:15**, (and how we will serve).

So how do we handle death? Scripture reminds us in **I Corinthians 15:55-57**, *"O death where is thy sting, O grave where is thy victory?"* We must understand who we are. We have to know that the real person is not the flesh and that the soul and spirit man on the inside will not die. Scripture further reminds us that, *"Absent from the body, and to be present with the Lord."* **(2 Corinthians 5:8 (KJV)**. Our last breath here is our first breath over there.

When we are convinced that we are not just placed in the ground and unconscious for a hundred years we will not fear death. Many people, including ministers, have given people a false message when it comes to death. These well-meaning persons will say things such as "God walked through the Garden, and picked your mother to complete his bouquet" or that "God needed a 'bud' when referring to your baby or child." **GOD IS CREATOR OF ALL!** He created the flower gardens and does not need to hurt us to "complete his bouquet."

John 10:10 (KJV) says, *"The thief cometh not, but for to steal, and to kill, and to destroy: I am come that they might have life, and that they might* *have it more abundantly."* Death is described as an "enemy." Only because Man sinned, does death have dominion in the earth. But Christ came to intercept Satan's plan and now, once again, we can live forever.

I am firmly convinced that Heaven is for real. Where there is joy and peace that far surpass what we classify as luxuries of this world. Recalling what my sister Sabrina said, "There is no house so beautiful, no marriage so perfect, and no kid so cute, that I need any of it." Yes, I felt offended at first, but then I looked at her statement in another way. The "house of your dreams" is never really that because you can always think of something you could change, add, or want more space. Not to mention there is always something breaking down, needing repair, needing to be painted, or simply just cleaned. As far as perfect marriages go, that doesn't exist. Yes, there can be good marriages between two people who love one another but it is work, and constantly evolving. Let's discuss children, they are not created perfect! LOL! Before I had my own children I would see couples or a mom with a baby in arms not realizing that the cute, dressed up baby just threw up on her, or she just changed a "poopy" diaper. Perhaps the father couldn't get any sleep and doesn't understand why the mother couldn't get the kid to shut up!

Welcome to the real world. Yes, I now understand what Sabrina meant but I thank God for what He's allowed me to enjoy in my life in this present world; despite that life is 80% - 90% work.

An acquaintance of mine, Kathy, passed away a few years ago. I was told that she was declared clinically dead. She said that she was in a place that was so beautiful. She remembered lying in deep, green, lush grass. When the Lord tapped her and told her that she would have to return to earth, she did not want to leave. She asked God to not have to deal with earthly problems if she came back but he did not make her that promise. He let her know that her mission on earth was not complete. When Sabrina sent us a message through Evangelist Luckie that there was so much, love, joy, and peace where she was it gave me hope that she was happy and her mission was accomplished even though I felt her stay on Earth was too short.. It gave me much comfort.

Recently my cousin Stephanie called me from Dallas, Texas. I was delighted to hear from her as it had been a while since we last talked. Stephanie was the one with my dad after he had ministered at church. She witnessed him take his last breath. I began to tell Stephanie that I was writing this book with a controversial topic. I told her that I attended a conference in New York in October 2016, when a Bishop from London spoke to me that I must complete the book that was on my heart by 2017. I explained to her that although I had made several attempts to write it, I had made very little progress due to my obligations, meetings and national and international travels. I was literally on "planes, trains, automobiles, and a ship"! So my plans to write had come to an abrupt halt.

I shared with Stephanie that on the morning of September 1, 2017 I was experiencing excruciating pain in my abdomen that was later diagnosed as Colitis. My husband insisted that I go to the Emergency Room. The pain was so intense that I was treated with morphine. I was told that I needed immediate surgery due to a bowel blockage. We began praying and asking God to help me. It had to be God's divine hand that caused the blockage to release because three days later I was sent home with antibiotics and pain medication and was told to follow-up with my doctor in two days. While on bedrest, I heard a voice say, "Now, you can write." I knew that meant to do what I was assigned to do now that I had the "down time."

We reminisced and she shared with me that two days prior to my dad's passing, they went to the cemetery where my mom and sister are buried next to one another. While approaching Sabrina's grave she could hear Sabrina's voice clearly in an excited child-like tone say, "Hi! Stephanie. It's so wonderful and beautiful here. Aunt Daisy, Aunt Florence, Mama, Big Mama, Big Daddy are all here, and John too." Stephanie later asked my other sister who John was. It took my sister a couple days to remember but John was our older cousin who had died years earlier in Fort Worth, Texas. We all had hoped that he made his peace with the Lord. This gave us the assurance that John had made it, indeed! The Bible lets us know in Psalms 116:15 (ESV) that "Precious in the sight of the Lord is the death of his saints." He has prepared a place for us where it is forever joy, and no memory of sorrow. We also discussed the night Dad passed after ministering at church. It was comforting to know that Stephanie was the person that was with him that Thursday night.

Bringing It Even Closer To Home

If I want to be more explicit, I can say, "Bringing it home then add closer." How much more home or closer can you get than your own household, namely your spouse. My husband, Truman, was the person I most feared when it came to sharing this project. Anyone who knows Truman (his name depicts who he is), knows he is a realist, no nonsense, black and white person. He should have been a lawyer instead of a dental surgeon. We are opposites. I am an adventurous person and trying new things (i.e. foods, rollercoasters. etc.) Truman keeps me grounded and I pull him out of the mud. It's true! Opposites do attract. It works well for us. I am sure your wondering how the two of us got together. I am from California and Truman is from Texas. We both know it was God-ordained. I was told the month and the day we would meet and the initials of his last name an "M" or "W." We met July 5th and married December 14th. We had only seen each other three time periods before our wedding. You are free to read the juicy details in my book *"Winning! By God's Grace in Satan's Face"*.

Did this unusual marriage work? Well, five children and nine grandchildren later, we are still together. According to my husband and soul mate, he says, we've never had a single argument. Then he laughs and says, "They are all doubles and triples." Early in our marriage we decided that no matter how much we disagreed we would always speak and respond to one another. We made another commitment that we would never threaten one another with the word DIVORCE. With the help of God, as we are both committed to Him, He has allowed our marriage to remain stable in spite of difficult seasons and situations. God is our peace in the midst of every storm.

On the train heading to a camp meeting on the Blackfeet Reservation in Montana, Truman asked, "What are you writing?" I thought, "Lord, how will I explain this to Mr. Logical?" However, to my surprise he opened up and shared some great information. Not only did he talk about biblical findings but he also shared about a friend and a patient that had had out of body experiences.

Like Pastor Joel Osteen says, I would like to share a funny story. Although "Doc", as we affectionately call him, can be a humorous and playful guy, he has a serious side and low tolerance for things that do not make sense or things that could be handled without a lot of drama. Here's a story for the record: Our oldest daughter, Tranisha, was asthmatic and had to take medication for her condition but she was also a "drama queen". This certain spring day I saw her coming down the street after getting off the school bus with an entourage of school kids behind her holding her books and sweater. She had her hands up to her forehead, struggling, huffing and puffing, as if she were on her last breath. The kids beat me to the door. They were shouting, "Mrs. Martin! Mrs. Martin! Tranisha can't breathe! Tranisha can't breathe!:" Yes my baby had asthma, but what apparently was a level 5, she had escalated to a 10. I gave her my "Mama look" and told the children thank you and sent them on their way. I took her things and said between my teeth, "Twinkie (her nickname), Get in here!" She panicked," Mama! Mama! I can't breathe!" I sat her down and gave her a breathing treatment and she recovered quickly. I thought, "Girl, I need to send you to Hollywood!" When her Dad came home that evening, her brothers, Trenton and Trevon, gave him the news on what occurred that day. He gave her a stern look and said, "Twinkie, you never lose it and walk down the street drawing all of that attention." Tranisha said, "Dad, I couldn't breathe. I thought I was going to die." (She thought that would get some sympathy from him). He replied, "Even if you die, die with dignity!" Now you can relate to why I went from fear to faith when dealing with my husband. But on the other side of his lion's roar is a very loving and kind-hearted person.

My husband shared an awesome story of one his patients. He was an elderly gentleman in his late 70's or 80's. He died at a church on Gettysburg Avenue not far from his dental office. Although there was no sign of life the paramedics kept working on him. In the meantime, the Saints were crying to God, "Please give him more time!" The man said he was gone away to a "Glorious Place" that was so beautiful that he could relate to the book *90 Minutes in Heaven*. He described it as a place of rest and peace where he was free from any worries. He described the fragrance and the beautiful flowers. He kept saying that he didn't want to return. This man, too, had an experience that proved that death is not just an empty, non-existent state. Jesus took the sting out of death. Blessed are those who die in the Lord.

Prior to his final heavenly journey, Doc also had the privilege of talking with Pastor Clyde Young the uncle of Mr. Curtis Pettis. He described his after-life experience as another dimension. He said he could see in 3-D. He could see through things. Not only could he hear music but he could see music as the scripture reminds us in **I Corinthians 2:9 (KJV),** *"But as it is written, Eye hath not seen, nor ear heard, neither have entered into the heart of man, the things which God hath prepared for them that love him."*

I had the awesome privilege of meeting young Reverend Logan Howard, of Washington, D.C. Logan was a young minister in his mid-20's and an extraordinary songwriter and musician. As renowned as he was, he never forgot The Great Commission of **Matthew 28:16-20 (KJV)**, not "The Great Suggestion." Also, in **Luke 14:23 (KJV)**, it commands us to: "Go out into the highways and hedges, and compel them to come in, that my house may be filled."

The reason I know that he did not forget The Great Commission is that Logan, a young man working on his dissertation at Howard University would invite students from campus to come to church. He even left gospel tracts in the restrooms on campus and my husband got one of those tracts. It was New Year's Eve when prior to going to a cabaret party, my husband went to the church Logan was a member of in order to appease his mom in Texas. While there he heard God's clarion call and went down to the altar and committed his life to Christ. Beyond just "joining church", he surrendered his will to the will and plan of God. Before leaving dental school he felt the call to ministry and the rest, as they say, is history.

What made me mention Logan? This awesome young man was diagnosed with lung cancer and went to be with Jesus at the early age of 25. A couple months before his departure, I had the opportunity to spend his last birthday with Logan and his family. He shared glorious stories of things he could see "over there." Both his and Pastor Clyde Young's experiences of hearing music intrigued me. The place was described as" glorious"! It was as if he could do a quick visit there, and then return back here to share, etc. Logan described the music as perfect pitch and harmony... perfect singing that was melodious!

Through Logan's sharing Jesus, not only did my husband receive Christ, but he went on to become a pastor, and is now a Bishop. He also travels to Africa and other countries and nations throughout the world. My husband is only one person of many that travel internationally to reach souls because of one young man with a passion for souls who was willing to obey God's call. He has stars in his crown, far beyond what I could have ever imagined! Logan will have so many stones in his crown that he will have to put them in a golden wagon and pull it behind him!

Another young man in his 40's, named Brian, also left a lasting impression on my husband's heart. He gave his testimony at my husband's brother's church in Southern California. Brian stopped by a gas station and to his surprise was approached by some gang members who needed to fulfill their gang initiation quota. This young man had the misfortune of showing up at "the wrong place at the wrong time". They shot five rounds of ammunition into his body and left him lying in a pool of blood on the pavement beside his car. As the paramedics picked up his body, he saw himself lying there in the pool of blood. As he hovered above, he could see them place his body on the gurney. He was baffled that he was actually alive, aware, and could see and hear what the paramedics were saying.

They rushed him by ambulance to the hospital and into emergency surgery. While recalling his statements, I am also aware that the "heavenly time zone" is different. It is timeless. He might have seen everything in a flash, *"in a moment, or in a twinkling of an eye."* **I Cor. 15:52 (KJV)**

Brian said that during the surgery he heard the doctors say, "We're losing him! Don't lose him! Let's try to save him and keep him here!" Then he heard another surgeon say, "He's gone." Someone else insisted that they continue with electrical shocks to his body. In the process he ascended into another dimension. It was glorious and bright! Total peace, love, and tangible joy! A presence was there as he started going towards the throne of God. He heard a voice coming from the throne saying, "Your work on Earth is not done." Then he began to descend back towards Earth. Brian said that although he loved his wife and children, he did not want to return. So much so, that he was trying to hold onto the clouds as he was descending. As he re-entered his body, his body shook with new life. He started to breathe, and his blood pressure began to stabilize. He could hear the surgeon say, "We got him back!" My husband said that the amazing thing was that he appeared fully recovered without any impairment or long-term effect. God allows people like Brian and others to get a "glimpse of glory" and to let us know that we do not have to fear because we have been created for eternity. What was lost in the Garden, as a result of disobedience, is now redeemed through Faith in Christ. We are redeemed from death and destruction.

In the Womb Versus Out of the Womb

My husband, Truman, made a profound statement: "Life and death reminds me of a baby coming out of the womb." In the womb, it's warm and comfortable for the most part. The baby lives effortlessly and all needs are met in this controlled environment. However, when it's time to be born and transition from that place of comfort, the baby is startled and cries. I am sure that if it could articulate, it would say, "Leave me here, I don't want to go."

Change and the unknown are challenges at any age or stage. Our lives can be compared to the baby coming out of the womb into the world during the birthing process. The baby enters a new environment quite different than the last nine months. The baby is embraced by this person he or she has never seen; the one who carried them. Although, unsure and apprehensive, and perhaps resistant when it enters this unknown world, the baby immediately begins to feel the essence of life. It is now no longer confined, but can move freely. It experiences new-found freedom in this big, new world. Its senses are acute and more sensitive to the new environment. If the baby, like Brian, could express himself, he it would not want to return to its linked and limited environment.

Life on Earth Versus Entering Heaven

Life on Earth is not to be compared to the Glory of Heaven that is to be revealed. Yet, we fear leaving here no matter how stressful and confining it may seem. Envision our limited view compared to the unlimited resurrected life God has for us. However, as Man, we still fear the unknown that we have yet to experience. When the time comes for us to transition from the familiar which we often refer to as the "good life" here on earth, we will enter into His glory. There we will experience pure joy, taste real freedom, have no more worries, stress; pain, nor fear as we see Jesus who gave his life for us, carried us, and redeemed us. We will feel like my parents, my sister, Logan, Brian, and your loved ones who do not want to return to this earth. Their last breath here was their first breath over there. And they are more alive than ever! They are now part of the "great cloud of witnesses" in "Heaven's Hall of Fame". Our loved ones are beckoning us to run the race and join them. We won't have to fear that day because we have God's promise.

As previously mentioned, my dad, Bishop Nathaniel Duffey, Sr., on a Thursday night, the 18th of August, walked into the church where he was Pastor, St. Paul Church of God in Christ, and taught and shared a sermon entitled: "Rest in the Lord" based on **I Thessalonians 4:13**. Upon completion, he gave instruction to his flock, and closed the service with the benediction and greetings. While sitting on the second row, in the middle section of the sanctuary he was transformed from his earthly house to his heavenly home. My dad knew his earthly body would rest from its stress, pain, and cares of this life. His conscious soul and spirit would embrace God's promises immediately until the day the body would be changed from mortal to immortal. Spirit, soul, and body would reconnect: "in a moment, in the twinkling of an eye." **I Cor. 15:52 (KJV)**. We can stand on God's promises in **Psalm 16:11 (KJV)**, "Thou will shew me the path of life: in thy presence is fullness of joy, at thy right hand are pleasures for evermore."It is also written in **Psalm 89:34 (Modern KJV)**, "I will not break my covenant, nor change the thing that has gone out of my lips."

God's Promises gives us hope when things are not seen... *"Now Faith is the substance of things hoped for, the evidence of things not seen."* **Hebrews 11:1 (KJV)**

Yes,

it

is

Far

Beyond

what

you

and I

can

see.

About the Author

Beverly Duffey-Martin, PhD., D.Min is an anointed, enthusiastic prophetic speaker, uniquely gifted.

"Dr. Bev" as she is affectionately called, is also an accomplished musician, songwriter, and singer. She has been featured on television programs, including TBN, which she has hosted on numerous occasions. She has authored an array of plays, poetry and has three albums to her credit.

Awards, Special Recognitions, & Affiliations

Dr. Bev's scope of ministry has taken her as far as India, Africa, Europe, Jamaica, Italy, Mexico, Korea and beyond. She has received numerous awards and recognition, e.g., at the invitation of Congressman Michael Turner, she was selected to participate in the Business and Professional Women's Leadership Summit in Washington, D.C.; was Keynote speaker for Dept. of Defense (Defense, Finance & Accounting Service); received City of Los Angeles Mayor's Certificate; on Sept. 11, 1993, donned "Beverly Duffey-Martin Day" by Mayor of City of Dayton, OH. Received certificates from The Ohio House of Representatives; State of Louisiana House of Representatives, Baton Rouge, Duly Commissioned Beverly Martin – Honorary State Representative Seal of Office in 1992.

Dr. Bev is an active member of the Links Incorporated. She served her local Chapter as Chaplin. She also served on the International Trends, Arts Scholarships and various other committees.

Educational Pursuits

Dr. Bev fulfilled most of her undergrad academia at Cal State University (CA), completing her last year at Central State University (OH), receiving a B.S. Degree in Education with a Music minor. She earned two master degrees: from IAU (Indiana) and the University of Dayton (OH). She received a PhD in Counseling from IAU. Dr. Bev also received a Doctor of Ministry degree from the United Theological Seminary, specializing in Administration of Urban Ministry and Church Development. Her project was Transitioning From Fragmentation of Rejection Towards Wholeness.

Special Assignments

Dr. Bev founded and directed the Women of Faith Power Network International, whose objective was to meet the total need of women within the body of Christ. She founded APW (Ask a Pastor's Wife), which provides support and fellowship for "First Ladies." She also founded Rays of Hope Network Inc., with a vision for women and youth especially disenfranchised young mothers.

In November 2015 she was appointed International Women's Supervisors of NAOFI (North American Outreach Fellowship International) in Buffalo, New York.

The Woman Behind the Ministry

Dr. Bev is the wife of Bishop Truman L. Martin, who is a dental surgeon as well as the Senior Pastor of Maranatha Worship Centre, in Dayton, OH. Dr. Bev serves alongside her husband as Administrator and Co-Pastor. She and her husband are the proud parents of five children: 3 sons and 2 daughters. Dr. Bev considers knowing Jesus and serving His people as one of her greatest joys in life.

First Book by Dr. Beverly Duffey-Martin

Available on Amazon in Paperback and Ebook

For additional information or to book Dr. Bev speaking engagements, please contact her at drbevphd@yahoo.com

CPSIA information can be obtained
at www.ICGtesting.com
Printed in the USA
FFOW03n1646150618
47115301-49617FF